The Happiness Solution:
Finding Joy and Meaning
In An Upside Down World

*May your life
be long + happy !
A lum Gettis, PhD*

Alan Gettis, Ph.D.

**GOODMAN BECK
PUBLISHING**

Cover photo © Zastavkin. Image from BigStockPhoto.com.

GOODMAN BECK
PUBLISHING
P.O. Box 253
Norwood, NJ 07648
www.goodmanbeck.com

ISBN 978-0-9798755-1-9
(previously published by Trafford Publishing ISBN 1-4120-1046-2)

Library of Congress Control Number 2008901870

Printed in the United States of America

10 9 8 7 6 5 4 3 2 1

Dedicated to my son, David,
and my daughter, Jenna,
who fill my life with
love, joy, and meaning.

Contents

Acknowledgements

I'd like to thank the many wonderful storytellers that have influenced me. They include Sheldon Kopp, Idres Shah, Joseph Campbell, and my father, George Gettis. Also, I owe a great debt to Zen literature and to the numerous Zen teachers and haiku poets I have learned from. Whenever possible, I have acknowledged the authors and storytellers responsible for material in this book. The book does contain folk tales and anecdotes of which I am unaware of any particular person being connected to. If I have failed to give an attribution when one was called for, I apologize, and future editions of this book will reflect appropriate acknowledgements. I am eternally grateful that I've been blessed with wonderful parents, extraordinary siblings, great friends, and my loving and beautiful wife, Nan. Thanks to my friend and colleague, Dr. Sam Menahem, for his feedback on drafts of this book, and to my pal, Dr. Joseph Luciani, for his ideas and enthusiastic support at every stage of this project. I also owe a debt of gratitude to my son, David, who did the typing, editing, and cover design, as well as offered many valuable suggestions.

Introduction

Speaking of the Kalahari Bushmen, Laurens Van Der Post said:

> The supreme expression of his spirit was in his stories. He was a wonderful storyteller. The story was his most sacred possession. These people knew what we do not: that without a story you have not got a nation, or a culture, or a civilization. Without a story of your own to live, you haven't got a life of your own.

Storytelling separates humans from beasts. People have been moved by stories for thousands of years. There were stories before Moses, Mohammed, Jesus, and Buddha. They have been handed down from tribe to tribe, from elders to youngers, from shamans, witches, priests, ministers, senseis, roshis, and rabbis. From time's inception, they have filled a universal need to connect us to our family, community, our universe, and to each other. Stories deal with our lives, our fallibilities, our joys and fears, our predicaments and our deaths. They also instruct, inspire, and point the way to fulfillment and the sacred.

This book is all about happiness. It examines what creates happiness and differentiates it from the societal myths that are associated with happiness – but are illusion. I've chosen to teach you about happiness by using stories because they evoke and nurture a part of the mind not reachable in more direct ways. These teaching stories sometimes contain implausible happenings that are meant to wake you from the slumber of your automatic instant replay day-to-day thinking.

The feedback from readers of my last book, *Seven Times Down, Eight Times Up: Landing On Your Feet In An Upside Down World*, confirmed what I already knew about teaching stories. Because they have multiple layers of meaning, and because the reader will resonate with them according to his or her readiness to receive the teachings, these stories may reveal different benefits to you with multiple readings.

In a 1919 paper entitled "The Uncanny," Sigmund Freud addressed this:

> ...the storyteller has a peculiarly directive influence over us; by means of the states of mind into which he can put us and the expectations he can rouse in us, he is able to guide the current of our emotions, dam it up in one direction and make it flow in another, and he often obtains a great variety of effects from the same material.

Or, as the poet-philosopher Gary Snyder put it, "Old tales and myths and stories are the koans of the human race."

When the great rabbi saw misfortune threatening the Jews, it was his custom to go into a certain part of the forest to meditate. There he would light a fire, say a special prayer, and a miracle would happen to avert disaster.

Many years later, his disciple had occasion, for the same reason, to intercede with heaven. He'd go to the same place in the forest and say, "Dear God. Listen! I do not know how to light the fire, but I'm still able to say the prayer." Again, the miracle would be accomplished.

Still later, a disciple of that rabbi who wanted to avoid misfortune for his people went into the forest and said, "I do not know how to light the fire, and I do not know the prayer, but I know this is the place and this must be sufficient."

Years later, the task of warding off tragedy fell to still another rabbi. Sitting in his armchair, his head in his hands, he spoke to God. "I am unable to light the fire and I do not know the prayer; I cannot even find the place in the forest. All I can do is tell the story, and this must be sufficient." And it was.

God loves stories.

I feel blessed that I have been able to be a full-time psychotherapist for the past 35 years. When I'm spouting long-winded psychological theories and explanations, I effect very little change in my patients. When I utilize compact teaching stories, it's a whole different ballgame. People may learn factual information via PowerPoint presentations, the Internet, lecturers, and even by looking at chalkboards, but life's most valuable lessons will be shared through stories. That's the way it's always been. Technology, as amazing as it is, will not change that. The human experience is within us, in our shared collective unconscious, waiting to be tapped into by teaching stories.

Tell me a fact and I'll learn.
Tell me the truth and I'll believe.
But tell me a story and it will live in my heart forever.
-Indian Proverb

Is it arrogant of me to write a book called, *The Happiness Solution*? I think not. Here's why:

-I've thoroughly researched happiness and what creates it.
-As a therapist, I continually work on helping others to remove obstacles to their happiness.
-I know what the key ingredients to the recipe for happiness are, and I want you to know them.
-I'm happy.
-I believe you can learn to be happier.

You are about to read a book based on my conviction that healing and happiness come in the form of stories, parables, and anecdotes. They will deal with your thoughts, feelings, behaviors, habits, and traits. They may challenge your beliefs regarding what is connected to happiness.

Happiness can be elusive. We have many millions of people suffering from various anxiety and depressive disorders. There is rampant drug abuse and alcoholism, and the divorce rate is skyrocketing. Prozac, Paxil, Xanax, and Ativan are as likely to be found in homes as are Tylenol and Tums. We are looking for happiness in all the wrong places. If you're unhappy, you're about to learn why and what you can do about it. If you're already happy, you're about to learn how to possibly be happier and experience more joy and peace of mind.

The Happiness Solution:
Finding Joy and Meaning
In An Upside Down World

The Stories

Singin' In the Rain

It was a dark and stormy night. Not really. I always joked that I would start a book with that sentence, so I did. Actually, it was a dark and stormy morning. I woke up a bit low on energy and with a dull headache. Debating whether to go to the gym or not, and still half asleep, I absent-mindedly bumped my head on the closet door. I'd been up only a few minutes and it was already turning into "one of those days." I was a bit less than a happy camper.

Still ambivalent about going to the gym, and on the border of indulging negative thoughts, I struck a compromise. I'd go to the gym, but I'd listen to the blues on my way there. So there I was, driving in a downpour with a landscape of endless gray, listening to Joe Williams wail out a song called, "Ain't Got Nothin' But the Blues."

Ain't got no tickle to fancy,
Ain't got no bounce in my shoes,
Ain't got no coffee that's perking,
Ain't got nothin' but the blues.

I put it on repeat and listened to it the whole ride to the gym.

As I signed in at the gym, Julie quickly entered me into the computer and matter-of-factly said, "You expire tomorrow."

Feeling like an old carton of milk, I queried, "My membership or me?" A line of a Lisa Loeb song ran through my mind:

I thought I'd live forever,
Now I'm not so sure.

I said to Julie, "I'm supposed to go to work in two hours. Since I expire tomorrow, do you think I should take today off?"

Julie responded, "I wouldn't go to work if I had only one day left to live. I'd party and do everything that I always wanted to do but never got the chance to."

7

I replied, "If it would only take you one day to do everything that you've always wanted to do, you've led quite a full life!"

I worked out for the next hour. Ran a bit. Pushed a few weights. Slowly began to feel more alive and ready to meet whatever the day had in store for me. When I was leaving the gym, I looked Julie in the eye, slowly shook my head from side to side, and playfully said, "Thanks for the expiration notice. Thanks a lot, Julie."

She feigned sadness and said, "I'll send a card to your family."

When I left the gym, the skies were already starting to clear. I didn't know how much time I had left, but I did know I was going to make the best of it. I can't sit around thinking about my expiration date. I have a life to live. I put on B.B. King.

> Hey everybody let's have some fun,
> 'Cause you only live once,
> And when you're dead you're done,
> So let the good times roll.

I put it on repeat and listened to it the whole way home.

Are You Happy?

Circle a number after each question. The higher the number circled, the more true the statement is as it applies to you.

(1) I tend to see the glass half-full rather than half-empty.
1 2 3 4 5
(2) I have very few regrets when I think about my life.
1 2 3 4 5
(3) I'm not a worrier. 1 2 3 4 5
(4) I frequently count my blessings. 1 2 3 4 5
(5) I have good friends. 1 2 3 4 5
(6) I feel loved by important people in my life. 1 2 3 4 5
(7) I sleep well. 1 2 3 4 5
(8) I am in relatively good health. 1 2 3 4 5
(9) I do not anger easily. 1 2 3 4 5
(10) I have people and/or activities in my life that I feel passionate about. 1 2 3 4 5
(11) I believe in a Higher Power or feel some spiritual connection to the universe. 1 2 3 4 5
(12) I like myself. 1 2 3 4 5

Score: Total _____

Interpretation:
12-24: Probably depressed.
25-36: Most likely unhappy.
37-47: Somewhat happy, but could be happier.

48-60: Life is good. You're most likely quite happy.

The Cardiff Giant

People believe what they want to believe regardless of whatever conflicting information is presented. That's the stuff of delusional systems. By definition, a delusion is a false belief that a person clings to despite any and all evidence to the contrary. O.J. Simpson and the jury. Need I say more?

The fossil of the Cardiff Giant was discovered in 1869. He was approximately 10 feet tall and his feet were 21 inches long. Word spread that the fossil was proof of the Bible's accuracy about giants such as Goliath. Stubb Newell, who owned the farm in Cardiff, New York, charged 50 cents if you wanted to get a look at the giant and take in a piece of Biblical history. Hundreds of people trekked daily from far and wide to the remote upstate New York farm. They came. They saw. And as we all know, seeing is believing. Isn't it?

As it turned out, the "fossil" was actually a carved slab of gypsum that was sculpted. George Hull, an atheist and businessman, and a distant relative of Newell, had spawned the hoax of the Cardiff Giant. Experts and scientists quickly declared it to be a fake, but that didn't discourage people from making the journey. In his book, *Frauds, Mysteries and Myths*, Kenneth Feder sums it up succinctly:

> Trained observers such as professional scientists had viewed the Giant and pronounced it to be an impossibility, a statue, a clumsy fraud, and just plain silly. Such objective, rational, logical, and scientific conclusions, however, had little impact. A chord had been struck on the hearts and minds of many otherwise level-headed people, and little could dissuade them from believing in the truth of the Giant. Their acceptance of the validity of the giant was based on their desire...to believe it.

What is your personal Cardiff Giant? What have you created and believe is reality that ultimately interferes with your joy and satisfaction? Is it real or is it something you believe so vehemently that nothing will get you to change your mind? This book is filled with new ways for you to think about yourself and your life and your happiness. As per Feder's references above, this book is filled with research, rationale, and scientific conclusions regarding how to be happier. But if you cling to irrational beliefs and self-defeating behaviors because you believe what you want to instead of what you need to, you are perpetuating your own personal hoax on yourself.

P.T. Barnum was never one to pass up a good thing when he saw it. He wanted to rent the Cardiff Giant for three months and take it on the road with his traveling circus. Newell and his business partners said no deal. The ever resourceful Barnum commissioned a duplicate giant to be carved and did make it part of the circus. So now, people were paying to see a fake of a fake. Interestingly enough, when both were displayed at the same time in New York City, Barnum's fake of the fake outdrew the real fake.

So we see once more that people believe what they want to believe. Do you believe you can be happier? Are you acting on that belief? What are you waiting for?

Remember Me?

It was Patriot's Day in Boston and it was cold. Just the way most of the runners preferred. The Boston Marathon would get underway in a few hours. Usually, Boston has about nine or ten thousand runners, but on this day there would be 40,000 in honor of the 100th anniversary of the marathon. I was one of those lucky enough to get in. More people got denied than were accepted. One hundred thousand runners would have presented somewhat of a logistical nightmare for the race organizers. It's a very hard race to manage normally, given that it starts in Hopkinton and ends 26.2 miles away in the heart of Boston. The extra 30,000 runners just turned a difficult situation into a more difficult one.

Hours before the 12:00 noon start, runners were roped off into outdoor corral type areas in relation to where they would start the race. I entered my designated area and began to ready myself for the event's start, which was still two and a half hours away. Being an experienced runner, I knew the tricks of the trade, and I had a good idea how to dress for the cold conditions. I brought old gloves and an old sweatshirt that I could warm up in and maybe even wear for a couple of miles before discarding. These "throw aways" are used by many runners. However, I did something for this run that I had never done before. I read a tip in *Runner's World* magazine that suggested wearing pantyhose to keep your legs warm. Yes, the tip was for men also. Although I decided that I wouldn't do the race in the pantyhose, I figured that I would wear them for those few pre-race hours that I'd be sitting around outside in the cold. In case you're curious, I have no history of or any interest in cross-dressing. Just wanted warm legs.

So it was that the evening prior to the marathon, my wife and I went to a store and she helped me pick out pantyhose. She suggested the queen size. I acquiesced. And that's how it came to pass that I was sitting in the corral at the Boston Marathon preparing myself to run – a six feet tall grown man with a beard, wearing tan queen size pantyhose. It was hectic and security was tight (not to mention my pantyhose). After an hour or more, I needed to get out of the roped off area. There were two burly, macho-looking Caucasian cops guarding the gateway. I approached one of them and asked if I could leave for a few minutes. I was concerned about being able to re-enter upon my return. I said to him, "Are you going to remember me, so I can get back in without any problems?"

He turned to the other cop and said, "Hey Mike, the guy in the pantyhose wants to know if we'll remember him!" They then shared a hearty laugh. That was the last time I wore pantyhose.

I think we all want to be remembered. How about the old television comedy, *Cheers*. The words in the theme song had to do with it being a bar "where everyone knows your name." And after we leave this earth, I think most of us want to be remembered. When my family lights the menorah at Chanukah (we celebrate most holidays), we always light a candle for our loved ones who have passed on. Gone, but never forgotten, we tell stories about them and remember them for their uniqueness and how they enriched our lives. And it is comforting to me to think that someday a candle will be lit for me. Hopefully. And, maybe my children or someone will tell a story about me and think of my uniqueness. And such is the power of stories and of traditions.

My wish for you is that you too will be remembered and someone will tell stories about you. But what kind of stories will they tell? That depends on how you live your life. How do you want to be remembered? You are in the process of writing your own story. It still has chapters to be written. Richard Bach once wrote, "Here is a test to find whether our mission on earth is finished. If you're alive, it isn't."

I hope some people remember me other than those two Boston cops. In the meantime, I'm heeding the words of the writer, George Sand:

> Try to keep your soul young and quivering right up to old age, and to imagine right up to the brink of death that life is only beginning. I think that is the only way to keep adding to one's talent, to one's affections, and to one's inner happiness.

Way To Go, Zoe

I've run a bunch of marathons. The first Olympic marathon was in Greece in 1896. It is a very time-honored event. If you have any physical or psychological vulnerability, it will probably manifest itself during a marathon. It's a bit like the Peter Principle. In other words, you work your way up until you reach your level of incompetence. You train hard and get better and better until you hit that point where your functioning is compromised. Something breaks down. Maybe it's your body, i.e. an ankle, blister, or knee, or maybe it's your mind. "I can't do this. What was I thinking? I'll never finish." Or, maybe it's your spirit. In any case, a marathon will teach you a lot about yourself.

The marathon was originally 25 miles. In 1908, Queen Elizabeth decided she wanted to watch the start of the event. To accommodate her, they moved the starting line back about 1.2 miles so that she could see the runners begin from her residence at Windsor Castle. That's how the marathon became a 26.2 mile run rather than the original 25 miles that Phidippides ran from the town of Marathon to Athens to announce the Athenian Army's victory in the Trojan War. An interesting footnote is that when he ran that distance and announced the victory, he keeled over and died. Such was the fate of the world's first marathoner.

You now have an appreciation for just how grueling the marathon can be, especially if it turns out to be on a hot, humid day. Once, I ran a winter marathon in a blizzard. Snow, ice, torrential winds and freezing temperatures. I somehow managed to get dehydrated and disoriented and wasn't quite sure where I was going. The halfway mark was at the same spot the run had started, so most of the runners stopped there. My body said, "STOP!" My mind said, "STOP!" Imagine my surprise when I kept going. I finished but have not run a marathon since. I ran marathons in the 1970's, 1980's, 1990's, and 2000's. Maybe that's enough. I'll think about it in 2010.

The majority of marathoners complete the marathon in about three and a half to five hours. Zoe Kaplowitz finished the New York City Marathon in 29 hours and 45 minutes. She was 55 years old. She did not sleep the entire time. Ms. Kaplowitz has had multiple sclerosis for over 30 years. She also has diabetes. Using two purple crutches, she literally inched her way all 26.2 miles. Every mile, she stopped to stretch. Every two hours, she tested her blood sugar to make sure her diabetes was under control.

Zoe Kaplowitz was dealing with reality and finding her own road to happiness. This was not Cockaigne. A Cockaigne is an imaginary land of ease and luxury. References to Cockaigne are prominent in Medieval European lore. There was a 13th century French poem called "The Land of Cockaigne" where "the houses were made of barley sugar and cakes, the streets were paved with pastry, and the shops supplied goods for nothing." Zoe knew different. She knew that life can be extremely difficult and that there's no such thing as a free lunch. Zoe knew that everyone dies, but not everyone lives.

Speaking of life and death, that same 2003 New York City Marathon had another story of courage and humanity. A 53 year old man with a 28 year old heart of a 16 year old finished the run. If that sounds confusing, let me help you sort it out. The man was close to death when, at age 41, he had a heart transplant. He received the heart of a 16 year old boy who was killed in an accident. So it was that 12 years later, the 53 year old man with the 28 year old heart of a 16 year old, completed the 26.2 mile road race. The man met the family of the donor and they all asked him if they could feel his pulse. Twelve years after they lost their loved one, they could still feel his heart beating.

In their landmark book, *Character Strengths and Virtues: A Handbook and Classification*, Christopher Peterson and Martin Seligman discuss how positive personality traits, called character strengths, are essential to our understanding of what contributes to well-being, fulfillment, and happiness. Seligman is the founder of the science of positive psychology. Positive psychology focuses on creating an optimistic approach to life rather than being obsessed with negativity, pathology, and mental disturbance. Many of his ideas and noted character strengths are woven into these stories.

One of the main character strengths has to do with courage. This has to do with not running away from feelings, but rather facing and dealing with challenges and pain. It has to do with acting on your own convictions. It has to do with hanging in there. It has to do with finishing what you start. It's about persistence and perseverance. It's about Zoe Kaplowitz. It's about the 53 year old man with the 28 year old heart of a 16 year old boy. It's about the boy's family. It's about you. And, it's also about our next story.

Caught Between a Rock and a Hard Place

On Saturday, April 26th, 2003, Aron Ralston went mountain climbing by himself in Canyonlands National Park in southeastern Utah. He was a very accomplished and experienced outdoorsman and climber. That area around Blue John Canyon is desolate and challenging, but the 27 year old Ralston had already scaled all 59 of Colorado's 14,000 foot peaks and was planning to tackle the 20,320 foot tall Mount McKinley, North America's highest mountain.

His Blue John Canyon trek was going to be a routine day trip and that's exactly what he packed for. He parked his pick up truck in a remote area and mountain biked 15 miles to the trailhead. He locked his bike to a Juniper tree and wearing just shorts and a t-shirt, he started his canyoneering. That's when a climber uses rock climbing skills, ropes, and gear to negotiate slot canyons. In his backpack were two burritos, water for the day, a small, cheap, dull and dirty knife, a digital camera, a camcorder, rock climbing gear, and a small first aid kit.

He wasn't due back to work until Tuesday and he hadn't told anyone where he was going. Aron Ralston, a man used to adventure and challenges, was about to embark upon more than he had bargained for. A massive 800 pound rock that he was maneuvering on as he was climbing down a ledge dislodged and pinned him in a three foot wide slot. He was in a standing position with his right arm pinned between the boulder and the canyon wall. He was trapped, literally caught between a rock and a hard place.

Ralston had been in jams before. He tried to remain calm and consider his options. He doubted someone would find him. The area was typically deserted. He thought about chipping away at the rock with his dull knife. He had one free arm with which to work. He wondered if he could rig up something with his limited gear that he could use to move the rock. He was an engineer by training and had a keen understanding of the mechanics of move-

17

ment. But within the first hour of being trapped, he understood that if all else failed, he would need to cut off his arm. He tried everything he could think of to move that boulder, but to no avail. Then, he chipped away at the gigantic rock for the next ten hours. He used that cheap knife and managed to produce a small handful of rock dust. In that standing position, unable to sleep, he continued working into Sunday and Monday to try to free himself.

Although Ralston was trying to conserve the burritos and water, by Tuesday he had nothing left to eat or drink. He finally tried to cut off his arm, knowing he would die in that spot if he couldn't free himself. The knife was so dull it could barely penetrate his skin. Even if it went through skin, tissue, and muscle, there was no way it would be able to cut through the bone and ultimately set him free. On Tuesday, his friends realized he may be missing and also notified his mother. Although no one knew where he went hiking, they tried to figure it out and a rescue effort began. Meanwhile, Ralston began to save his urine.

On Wednesday, he began to drink his urine in an effort to stay alive. He was dehydrated and flirted with delirium. Although Ralston had exhausted his food, water, and supplies, one thing remained – his will to live. He would do whatever it took. He valued being alive and never gave up hope. But just in case, he pulled out his video camera and recorded a message to his parents. Then, on the canyon wall, he etched his name and date of birth and wrote R.I.P. He knew it was possible that this could be his last day alive.

It wasn't. On Thursday, the 6th day of his entrapment, Ralston had a vision of a three year old boy running across a sunlit floor to be scooped up by a one-armed man. He believed this was his future son. He knew it was time to take drastic action. Despite waning strength, he began cutting off his right arm. Because of the decomposition of tissue, the dirty, dull knife was able to cut more effectively. But realizing it wouldn't be able to cut through the bone, Ralston forced his arm into the boulder so as to break the radius bone and ulna. Then, he made a tourniquet and amputated his right arm below the elbow. He was free. Leaving his arm behind, he rigged anchors and rope and garnered his remaining strength to climb out. He then hiked five miles to Horseshoe Canyon and encountered a Dutch family. They aided him and were instrumental in his eventual rescue by helicopter, although he essentially saved himself. Later, it would take heavy equipment and 13 men to retrieve the severed arm.

When people that I work with are in difficult situations, I remind them again and again that they are capable of handling them. When they tell me how hard it is, I acknowledge it, but tell them, "You can do hard things." Aron Ralston decided to do whatever it took to stay alive – that was his goal. This book will be like the old knife that he used. It is the tool that will do it for you if you have the ingenuity, open-mindedness, and courage to act on the insights provided here. If your goal is to be happier, are you willing to do whatever it takes? Will you do the equivalent of whatever it means for you to drink your own urine and cut off your own arm?

What's It All About, Alfie?

At some point in a person's life, she or he may question whether there's any point of existing. Peggy Lee sang that infamous refrain, "Is that all there is?" And how about the movie and song *Alfie*, which both query, "What's it all about, Alfie?" Sometimes, people conclude life is meaningless or absurd.

What if the Hokey Pokey really is what it's all about?

Not being able to find ultimate meaning or absolute answers does not render life meaningless. It does not equate to absurdity. I believe in life before death. I hope you do too. Create meaning and purpose. Strive for an existence characterized by a degree of intensity and depth, which gives rise to feelings of fulfillment. The alternative is to go through life in the deathlike "Is that all there is?" position.

There is a famous experiment in quantum mechanics that was done in 1935 by Erwin Schrodinger, the distinguished physicist. It can be summarized as follows:

> First, we have a living cat and place it in a thick lead box. At this stage, there is no question that the cat is alive. We then throw in a vial of cyanide and seal the box. We do not know if the cat is alive or if it has broken the cyanide capsule and died. Since we do not know, the cat is both dead and alive, according to quantum law, in a superposition of states. It is only when we break open the box and learn the condition of the cat that the superposition is lost, and that cat becomes one or the other (dead or alive).

So, Schrodinger's cat is actually in an indeterminate position of being possibly alive and dead at the same time. This experiment created so much confusion in quantum physics that Schrodinger once quipped that he's sorry he ever met that cat.

The brilliant, analytical theorist, Erich Fromm, brings related issues closer to home. He believed that man's basic alternative is the choice between life and death, and that every action reflects this choice:

> Life and death, as spoken of here, are not the biological states, but states of being, or relating to the world. Life means constant change, constant birth. Death means cessation of growth, ossification, and repetition. The unhappy fate of many is that they do not make the choice. They are neither alive nor dead.

In essence, they become Schrodinger's cat.

Dr. Dan Baker, the director of the Life Enhancement Program at Canyon Ranch, differentiates the "emotionally enhanced life" from the "lesser life."

The Emotionally Enhanced Life Is characterized by:	The Lesser Life Is characterized by:
*Love	*Fear
*Health	*Illness
*Optimism	*Pessimism
*Spirituality	*Spiritual emptiness
*Courage	*Cowardice
*Altruism	*Self-involvement
*A sense of freedom	*A lack of options
*Perspective	*A narrow focus
*Proactivity	*Passivity
*A good sense of humor	*A poor sense of humor
*Security	*Anxiety and depression
*Purpose	*Purposelessness

In his recent book, *What Happy People Know*, Dr. Baker relates brain physiology and evolution to our quest to be happy. The brain stem, also known as the reptilian brain, was the first part of the brain to evolve in animals, 100 million years ago. It's all about instinctual fears and survival. The reptilian brain is incapable of higher thought. It produces the classic fight or flight or freeze response to stress. The last part of the brain created during evolution, and the last part of the brain developed in the womb, is the neocortex. Fortunately, the neocortex can overrule the reptilian brain's fear system by utilizing intellect and spirit. The "emotionally enhanced life" characterized above comes about when we are able to harness the neocortex to manifest those 12 qualities listed. If we do not do that, we will be governed by the fear of not having enough and not being enough. The result will be the 12 qualities cited under the "lesser life."

So, "What's it all about, _____?" (Please fill in the blank with your name.) It appears that a large part of what it's about is paradoxical. It's about facing your fears while realizing your uniqueness and passionately discovering your individuality.

If you do not get it from yourself,
where will you go for it?

If not now,
when?

It's also about transcending individuality to experience spirituality, wonder, mystery, and the connectedness of the universe.

Day after day the sun rises in the east.
Day after day it sets in the west.

A Matter of Perspective

For much of my life, I labored under the delusion that I knew best. If it came down to considering doing it your way, her way, their way, or my way, I'd almost always conclude that my way was the best way. Suffice it to say, I now realize I wasn't the most objective judge. I'm now a lot less cocky and considerably more happy. I think there's a relationship between the two.

> There's more than one way to skin a cat.
> -Folk wisdom

Not jumping to conclusions, not staunchly defending your take on things, being able to truly listen to and appreciate others' positions, and being able to change your mind are all related to the trait of open-mindedness. My cat (who is not named Schrodinger) and I have engaged in a ritual for the past 16 years. A few of us in the family eat egg whites. I'll frequently make a batch of hard-boiled eggs. Every time I crack the eggs to peel them, Mittens magically appears. It doesn't seem to matter where she is in the house or whether she's awake or asleep. The sound immediately rouses her and she comes to the kitchen and leans against my leg. She is our cat but is also Pavlov's dog. She'll meow and stare at me, pleading her case to get an egg yolk.

Most of the time, I'll acknowledge her by talking sweetly to her and I'll give her an egg yolk. This almost daily ritual of many years duration is quite interesting, because the kicker is that she never eats the egg yolk. She'll sniff it. Occasionally, she'll roll it a little by pushing it with her nose or tongue. After about 10-15 seconds, she'll lose interest and walk away. My wife and I never cease to be amazed. We used to think she was just slow and not very bright. Then, we concluded it must not be the result that's important to her. Maybe it's all about the process. After all, she does manage to get some sweet talk and push around an egg yolk. Maybe whether she likes and/or eats the yolk is not what it's about. All we know is that if we crack open a hardboiled egg, Mittens will come. In fact, on rare occasions when she's been unaccounted for for too long a time, we've cracked an egg to crack the case of her disappearance. To be honest, I don't really know what the ritual is about. I'd be just as open to your thoughts on the matter as my own.

If we are more open-minded, we're less likely to feel frustration and anger. We're also less likely to feel misunderstood and disappointed. If we rigidly stick to the idea that we know best, we're setting ourselves up for power struggles, controlling behaviors, and defensive postures. Keep in mind that much of the time, it's less an issue of right or wrong and more a matter of perspective.

Times were rough in the village. The keeper of the monkeys was instructed to reduce the ration of nuts. He told the monkeys, "It will be three nuts in the morning and four in the evening." The monkeys were furious. "Very well then," he said. "You shall have four nuts in the morning and three in the evening." The monkeys accepted with delight.

"Aha!" The light bulb went off. For 16 years, I've given Mittens the yolks. She's never eaten one. She probably wants the egg white, not the yolk. Today, her persistence would finally be rewarded. I cracked the egg. She came. She meowed. She pawed at my leg and looked at me hopefully. And this time, instead of the yolk, I gave her the white. And, of course, you know what happened. She sniffed it, pushed it a bit, and walked away.

Blah Blah Blah

Let me get right to the point. One of the main causes of your unhappiness is the incessant self-chatter you engage in. Not out loud. In your mind. It is akin to a preoccupation with yourself. You may even consider it a strength. Perhaps you describe it as being introspective or analytical. This steady stream of concern with evaluating yourself and your life leads to being overly self-conscious, having poor interpersonal relationships, anxiety, and/or depression. The self-chatter can interfere with memory, attention span, sexual performance, sleep, job performance, and judgment.

Sometimes the self-chatter takes the form of "what ifs." For example, "What if she doesn't like my proposal?" or "What if I have a panic attack?" or "What if I never meet my soul mate?" Sometimes, the "if onlys" take over. "If only I had enough money, I could..." or "If only my nose was small, I'd..." and so on. We also have the "I could have," "I should have," the "Yes, but," and the "I wish" variations.

In the late 70's, when American cars were not in such great demand, there lived a man who owned a Chrysler dealership in a small town in the Midwest. This guy was not doing so well. He saw his competitors selling Hondas, Toyotas, and other Japanese cars, with customers lining up to buy their small gas efficient vehicles, while he whiled away his time pining for even one person to enter his dealership to examine his gas guzzlers. Anyway, one day he went fishing and caught this little goldfish who, to his surprise, said, "Please sir, I am a special fish with magical powers. Let me go and I'll give you one wish." The guy thought to himself, "What have I to lose?" and let the fish go free. The fish thanked him and told him to write his wish on a piece of paper and put it under his pillow and sleep on it. In the morning, his wish would be fulfilled. So that night, the guy wrote, "I wish to own a foreign car dealership in a large cosmopolitan city." He put the paper under his pillow and the last thing he thought before going to sleep was, "Here goes nothing." The next morning he woke up in Tokyo owning a Chrysler dealership. As the old saying goes, be careful what you wish for.

But back to self-chatter leading to unhappiness. It is imperative that you work on reducing all the blah blah blah. Learning to quiet your mind and feel calmer and happier is doable and essential to your mental health. Most of the thoughts you generate are probably not in the service of your feeling content. Catch yourself when you are over-thinking or indulging unnecessary thoughts. Visualize yourself putting your index finger to your mouth and gently saying, "Sssshhhh." Quiet yourself down. Learn to produce fewer unproductive thoughts. Thoughts can be characterized as being toxic or nourishing. Put up that "stop" sign when toxic thoughts are recognized. Simply let them go by shifting your consciousness to whatever you are actually doing at that time, i.e., tasting pizza or listening to John. Nourishing thoughts are fine, but the rule in general is don't overfeed yourself. It's not a good idea to stuff yourself with toxic or nourishing thoughts. Stuffing yourself with either equals self-preoccupation. Too many thoughts in and of themselves can be stressful. It's sort of like being exposed to noise all day long.

You can get better and better at reducing self-chatter by practicing.

Young Man: "Excuse me, sir. How do I get to Carnegie Hall?"
Old Man: "Practice, practice, practice."

Mental health skills are similar to other skills. If you wanted to be a better tennis player, it would help to take a few lessons and then practice your strokes by hitting hundreds and hundreds of tennis balls. If you want to feel happier, you have to practice the skills related to it. When you become conscious of self-chatter, don't indulge it. Let it go and quiet down. Don't be hard on yourself if this process doesn't come easily to you. You're used to attending to the noise. It may feel awkward when you practice non-attending. Don't get discouraged.

The person who removes a mountain
begins by carrying away small stones.
-Chinese Proverb

Sssshhhh. Less noise. Less pre-occupation with yourself. "Stop" sign. Change the channel. Keep it simple.

I always listen for what I can leave out.
-Miles Davis

The Hundredth Monkey

The New Age author, Ken Keyes, Jr., has written a treatise entitled *The Hundredth Monkey*. It refers to experiments on monkeys living in northern Japanese islands in the 1950's. The original research reported by Lyall Watson in his book *Lifetide* espoused the notion that when enough people hold something to be true, it becomes true for just about everybody. Although it sounds implausible, it's an interesting idea to ponder. Great thinkers in other fields have put forth similar theories. For example, Carl Jung's collective unconscious with the concept of archetypes and Sheldrake's Theory of Morphogenetic Fields could lend credence to the hundredth monkey phenomenon.

Here's what happened in 1952 on the island of Koshima. Scientists gave monkeys sweet potatoes that were dropped in the sand. The monkeys enjoyed the taste of raw sweet potatoes but not the sand. Imo, an 18 month female monkey discovered that she could wash the sand off the sweet potatoes by putting them in a nearby stream. She taught her mother. She also taught her playmates. In turn, they taught their mothers. Slowly but surely, this innovation was learned by many other island monkeys. Between 1953 and 1958, all of the young monkeys learned how to wash the sand away. Adult monkeys who didn't imitate their children continued to eat dirty sweet potatoes.

Nothing too unusual so far. Just standard principles of learned behavior. But here's where things get interesting. It was in the autumn of 1958 when the hundredth monkey phenomenon evidenced itself. Keyes writes, "Let us suppose that when the sun rose one morning, there were 99 monkeys on Koshima Island who had learned to wash their sweet potatoes. Let us further suppose that later that morning, the hundredth monkey learned to wash potatoes. THEN IT HAPPENED! By that evening, almost everyone in the tribe was washing sweet potatoes before eating them. The added energy of this hundredth monkey somehow created an ideological breakthrough!"

It doesn't stop here. It gets even more interesting. Keyes continues, "But notice. A most surprising thing observed by these scientists was that the habit of washing sweet potatoes then jumped over the sea. Colonies of monkeys on other islands and the mainland troop of monkeys at Takasakiyama began washing their sweet potatoes!" In essence, this was a spontaneous transmission of a belief/behavior across space without direct physical contact. So, supposedly, when a "critical mass" point is reached, a new awareness can be communicated directly from mind to mind.

I'm not sure if there indeed can be some mysterious transformation of consciousness as per the teaching of that critical mass or energy field. I'm not that interested in analyzing it critically or even taking it so literally. There's just something about it that exudes hope and transcendence. I kind of like the concept even if it seems a bit naïve to do so. It reminds me of the research that shows when people are prayed for (without their knowledge) by many other people, their outcomes are better than those who are not prayed for.

Is part of the happiness solution teaching enough people to be happy so that some critical mass is reached and happiness spreads from consciousness to consciousness? Well if you are happier, your family, friends, coworkers, and others you come in contact with may be happier. And they'll affect those they're in contact with. And then, in a manner of speaking, the hundredth monkey will be affected. And then...

So, whether you're a monkey learning to do what it takes to have a better tasting sweet potato, or a human learning what it takes to be a happier person, don't underestimate the tremendous impact your efforts may have on your life and on the world at large. Be the hundredth monkey!

> We become like ancient Chinese teapots. When a beloved teapot is used by a Chinese family for a hundred years or more, it is said, there is no need to put in tea. You just pour in water and the pot makes tea by itself.
> -Jack Kornfield

If Only...

We are a society that values "more." The more the better. Bagels no longer have holes in them and are about the size of those donut spare tires that come with most new cars. Speaking of "new," we also have a penchant for the newest and the best. The bigger the better. The more the merrier. The newer the nicer. We're seeking the latest, the new and improved, the cutting edge, the cat's meow, and the state of the art. We want successful careers, meaningful relationships, family, the new Lexus, large screen plasma TV's, nirvana, and a minimum of 15 minutes of fame. We want things to be different than they are. We want things to be better. We want to look different, vacation in Hawaii, and make more money. We want the Norman Rockwell Thanksgiving. This is just the short list for starters. We want better sex, more power and prestige. We want it all.

There's probably no better symbol for our philosophy and consumerism than the mall. We are surrounded by them, and in turn, they surround us with things that we seemingly need to have. The irreverent comedian, George Carlin, has a whole routine about our "stuff." It's quite hilarious. It's also true. We buy more and more stuff until we've got stuff all over the place and are running out of room for all our stuff. On top of that, we go to garage sales and buy other people's stuff; the stuff they no longer want but we think we can't live without.

We are the ultimate consumers. Madison Avenue has done its job admirably. If we are to be happy, we need to look a certain way, smell a certain way, and wear the clothes of certain designers. We have to possess certain items and go to certain places. We have to drive certain vehicles and drink certain drinks. All of this is supposed to guarantee our happiness. I wouldn't be so certain. In fact, it may be that our compulsive acquiring of goods and services takes us in the opposite direction. Always having to have the latest and greatest can lead to a sense of never quite being satisfied with what you have.

When televisions were first introduced, those fortunate enough to be able to own one had black and white sets with about seven inch screens. There were only a few network channels. There was static and the picture would periodically reflect both vertical and horizontal fluttering and distortions. Families would typically gather around the TV and watch shows together. In my youth, we had seven channels to choose from, and we needed to get up and go to the TV to adjust the volume or change the channel. We were happy with that small screen black and white TV and the few channels we had.

Fast forward to 2006. If we have a 20 inch color television, we yearn for a 24 inch or a 27 inch one. If we have a 27 inch TV, we feel the need for a 27 inch flat panel TV. If we have a 27 inch flat panel, we may feel frustration that it's not equipped with surround sound or doesn't have a picture in picture feature. Flat panels may not be good enough. There's high definition TV, combo TV/VCR/DVD systems, and Dolby sound. What used to seemingly make us happy doesn't anymore. But, if we can only get that 60 inch plasma TV, we know we'll be happy. Oh yeah?

Unlike the seven channel situation of my youth, we now have cable television and hundreds of channels. But we're not quite satisfied with all those channels. We'll be happier with enhanced cable, HBO, and other assorted extras. Channel surfing from our couches with our remotes is the order of the day. My generation gets quite confused with the four or five remotes on the family room coffee table. In a senior moment, I once picked up a remote and tried to make a phone call. Do all of these technological advances make us happier? I think not. The younger generations are growing up with a sense that they need all the latest and best of everything. They are growing up with a sense of entitlement and with the philosophy that material possessions bring happiness.

This can get pretty absurd. A guy who owns a small jet wishes he owns a bigger one. The teacher wishes she was a principal. The principal wishes she was a superintendent. The priest wishes he was a bishop. The bishop wishes he was pope. I think it's a wonderful thing to have aspirations, goals, and drive. But, sometimes it's important to recognize when enough is enough. What will it take for you to feel satisfied with who you are and what you have?

One day, Nasrudin went walking and found a man sitting on the side of the road. The man was sobbing.

"Why are you crying?" asked Nasrudin.

"Because I'm so poor," said the man. "I have no money. Everything I own is in this little bag."

"Ah-ha!" exclaimed Nasrudin, and he quickly grabbed the bag and swiftly ran away until he was out of sight.

"Now I have nothing," cried the poor man as he slowly walked in the direction Nasrudin had gone. About a mile or so down the road, he discovered his bag sitting at the roadside. He became ecstatic. "Thank God!" he screamed. "I have all my possessions back. Thank you, thank you!"

"Hmmmmm!" exclaimed Nasrudin, appearing out of the bushes by the side of the road. "Isn't it interesting that the same bag that made you weep now makes you so happy."

-Sufi Story

Consider this simple but remarkable premise. Happiness isn't so much about getting what you want as it is about wanting what you have. Happiness isn't so much about getting what you want as it is about wanting what you have. (Yes, I wanted to write it twice, for emphasis!) In fact, Dr. Timothy Miller has written an entire book devoted to this idea. It's entitled, *How To Want What You Have*. If we stop craving for more, bigger and better, we will suffer less (as pointed out so succinctly in Buddha's Four Noble Truths). You don't need the best body, the most money, the nicest house, or to travel to the ends of the earth in order to be happy. Happiness is a way of traveling, not a destination. If you are more accepting of who you are and what you have, you will feel more satisfied. If you always crave what you don't have, you will continue to feel frustrated and disappointed. Try letting go of your notions about what you should have and learn to want what you do have.

It's important to learn that enough is enough and that more is not necessarily better. Get better at saying no to yourself. As you continue to say no, your self-respect will grow. Life will become a bit less complicated. You'll need less room for your stuff and you'll travel a little lighter. You will become more disciplined and less overwhelmed. Be thankful for what you have and stop craving for what you don't have. Your happiness depends upon it.

Mending Fences

A handful of patience is worth more
than a bushel of brains.
-Dutch Proverb

One of the first prominent American psychologists, William James, said that the art of being wise is the art of knowing what to overlook. Feeling and expressing anger in a rageful way typically runs counter to happiness. When one person belittles or demeans another, both parties suffer consequences such as lowering of self-esteem, discouragement, and guilt. A Chinese axiom is, "If you are patient in one moment of anger, you will escape a hundred days of sorrow."

When I work with people who anger easily, I begin by educating them as to the destructive aspects of doing so. Their fury can erode or even destroy relationships while fostering an out-of-control feeling in themselves. Then I attempt to help them learn how to control their impulses to lash out by pausing, re-thinking things through, and using self-talk to bring about different behaviors. We talk about building a longer fuse and try to discover the reasons they have had so much difficulty with their tempers.

We talk about the importance of becoming less reactive by learning to be better listeners. I try to get them to develop the capacity to put themselves in the other's shoes and try to understand things from that perspective. No matter what someone says to them, I tell them it is their own response that is crucial. A Japanese saying is, "The second sentence makes the quarrel." I tell them to remind themselves that they have two ears and one mouth and should listen twice as much as they speak. And, I urge them not to speak unless it is an improvement on the silence. In other words, it's about understanding the power of words and not using them as ammunition. You don't always have to be right or have the last word. It's not about winning or losing. It's better to be kind than to be right. Being kind is directly related to the degree of happiness you will feel.

There was a little boy with a bad temper. His father gave him a bag of nails and told him that every time he lost his temper, to hammer a nail in the back fence. The first day the boy had driven 37 nails into the fence.

Then it gradually dwindled down. He discovered it was easier to hold his temper than to drive those nails into the fence. Finally the day came when the boy didn't lose his temper at all. He told his father about it and the father suggested that the boy now pull out one nail for each day that he was able to hold his temper.

The days passed and the young boy was finally able to tell his father that all the nails were gone. The father took his son by the hand and led him to the fence.

He said, "You have done well, my son, but look at the holes in the fence. The fence will never be the same. When you say things in anger, they leave a scar just like this one. You can put a knife in a man and draw it out. It won't matter how many times you say 'I'm sorry,' the wound is still there."

Be kind, for everyone you meet
is fighting a battle.
-Plato

For Members Only

You didn't get all you wanted. Your needs weren't always met. Plenty of times you got what you didn't want. Your childhood was a nightmare. You've suffered serious losses. You've felt inadequate, inferior, and insecure. Sometimes you felt like an imposter. You've felt frightened. You've felt misunderstood, frustrated, and disappointed. You're aging rapidly.

So, is it none of the above, two of the above, all of the above? My guess is that it's, at the minimum, some of the above. Well, welcome to the club! And here's the kicker – no one is immune. We might be on different time tables, but we all get a turn struggling mightily with life's inherent issues. There is no escape. No exit. If you spend time thinking that you're always getting the short end of the deal, that the grass is indeed greener on the other side of the fence, and that you'd be better off being someone else, you're wrong.

We're all in the same club. I like to think of it as "Our Gang." Remember those scruffy kids? Alfalfa, Buckwheat, and the others. Quite a collection of characters, but all in the same gang. That's what we have. The threatening looking guy on the motorcycle with the tattoos, your neighbor in the bigger house with the expensive sports car, your priest, your garbage man, the lead actors in your favorite television drama or sitcom, the mayor of your town, the guy who trades your stocks and the person who you saw shoveling the elephant dung at the circus are all in the same gang as you. Me too. And even that rude woman who came from the other direction and pulled right into that parking spot you'd been waiting for. Yup, her too. Everybody's in the club. Everyone's fighting something, trying to get their needs met, and trying to find happiness.

We've all had our share of tragedy, embarrassment, fear, anxiety, guilt, and anger. We've all been let down. No one is above the fray. It may look like it, but that's not the reality. It's a masquerade. Externals don't portray insides. We're all part of "Our Gang."

Instead of continuing to dwell on the idea that you have gotten a raw deal, that life is unfair and that others lead charmed lives, how about dwelling on what you need to do now in order to begin to feel better. It's never too late to begin. You can start to live the life you want. Let go of your negativity. What do you have to lose? Only your unhappiness.

We either make ourselves happy or miserable.
The amount of work is the same.
-Carlos Casteneda

The Present

We pay lip service to the idea of living in the present. We've all heard the advice to take time to smell the roses and wake up and smell the coffee. We've heard it, but that's about it. I'd like you not only to hear it, but to let it sink in fully, into your bones and into your marrow. I'd like you not only to digest it, but to live it and breathe it. If there's anything resembling a magic bullet or a key to the universe, it's the ability to be fully present in a non-self-conscious way here and now.

To the degree that you spend time worrying about your yesterdays or your tomorrows, your happiness will be affected. If you are spending your time being both regretful about and disappointed with your past, you will not be happy now. If you spend a lot of time being frightened of and worried about your future, it will be hard for you to appreciate that you are capable of being happy now.

In his landmark book *The Farther Reaches of Human Nature*, Abraham Maslow writes about muga, which is a Japanese word that describes present moment awareness. It "...is the state in which you are doing whatever you are doing with total wholeheartedness, without thinking of anything else, without any hesitation, without any criticism or doubt or inhibition of any kind whatsoever. It is pure and perfect and total spontaneous acting without any blocks of any kind." We've all had those flow experiences in which we've lost ourselves in an activity or a conversation and we simply felt good and alive. There was no process of self-evaluation taking place, no pre-occupation with how we're doing or how we will be graded. In those flow experiences, there was no past and no future. You were simply living fully in that moment at that time.

Robert K. Cooper addresses this admirably in his book *Health and Fitness Excellence: The Scientific Action Plan*:

> May you always remain aware that the greatest contribution you can make – to yourself, to your loved

ones, to your work, to humanity – begin, are nurtured, and are expressed right now, right now, right now...because *right now* is the only time on earth that is ever truly yours.

A Zen Master lay dying. One of his disciples, recalling the fondness that his teacher had for a certain cake, went in search of some in the bake shops of Tokyo. After some time, he returned with the delicacy for the master, who managed a feeble smile of appreciation and slowly nibbled at it while moving closer to death with each small bite. His student asked if he had any departing words for them. He whispered, "Yes." They drew closer, so as not to miss the faintest syllable. He said, "My, this cake is delicious!"

Yesterday is history.
Tomorrow is a mystery.
Today is a gift.
That's why it's called 'the present.'
-Author unknown

Coffee, Anyone?

In Cape Cod this past summer, I discovered a little hole-in-the-wall Brazilian bakery. I've always had a penchant for strong coffee. One cup a day is plenty for me, but I look forward to that cup. I'm not addicted. Sometimes I go weeks without having any. But for me, coffee is one of the small pleasures of life. When I saw the bakery, the line of an old song began running through my head. I'm not sure about the name of the song, but I think it's called "The Coffee Song." It may have been by Sinatra. The line of the song as I remember it is, "They make an awful lot of coffee in Brazil!" I'm pretty sure it's something like that. Anyhow, this refrain seemed to get stuck in my brain circuitry and I was humming it and singing it for a good deal of the summer. Luckily, it felt like an unobtrusive obsession and I felt fine whenever it showed up. "They make an awful lot of coffee in Brazil!" There it goes again.

Back to the story of the little Brazilian bakery. As I entered the place, which was painted a pale lime green, I encountered the store owner. He nodded. I asked something along the lines of, "What kind of coffee do you have?" He pointed. I looked in the direction his finger indicated and there it was. One coffee pot. That was it. Wait a minute. Was that really it? It was true. There was no decaf. No latte. No French vanilla, hazelnut, or chocolate raspberry. There was no dark roast , morning blend, or Ethiopian organic. No cappuccinos. No espressos. There was just a pot of coffee. Take it or leave it. Well, since I'm pretty much of a no frills guy and happen to like a strong cup of black coffee, this was fine by me. In fact, it was more than fine.

Life has seemingly gotten more hectic and more complicated with each decade. As a kid, if I needed sneakers, they were black or white and were Keds or Converse. That was it. Now, buying sneakers is like buying a car. The options with colors and styles and heel gels and, well, you get the idea. Sometimes things are more complicated than they need to be. The simplicity of the Brazilian bakery was akin to a bit of an oasis in the midst of our hurried lives. The store carried five or six different types of baked goods and rolls. They all looked interesting although I wasn't quite sure what any of them were.

I got a cup of coffee to go. They only offered one size cup. No small, medium, large, extra large, grandee, or fire hydrant size. Just a regular size cup. The owner spoke very little English but we communicated just fine. I pointed to a slice of something that looked like corn bread and said, "I'll have one of those." Then, I pointed to a small, round baked item about the size of a golf ball and asked for two of those. He gave me everything in a previously used brown paper bag.

"Three dollars," he said.

Later that morning I savored the coffee and shared the baked goodies with my wife. They hit the spot. Much of the day I was singing, "They grow an awful lot of coffee in Brazil!" Sometimes it was "grow" and other times it was "make." Sometimes I'd sing it silently but other times I'd belt it out. After awhile, my wife was singing it too.

The next morning, I returned to the bakery, and after exchanging good morning smiles and nods with the owner, I bought a cup of coffee, three fairly large rolls, and something that resembled a single serving size of pie.

"Three dollars," said the proprietor.

The following day, I got my cup of coffee and six of those golf ball sized things. When the owner asked for three dollars, I began to wonder if this was simply coincidental or not. I ordered something different on each of the next ten days. I changed the number of items, ordering as few as two and as many as seven. He always charged me three dollars. It worked for him and it worked for me. Whenever I was in the Brazilian bakery, life seemed simpler and easier. I think the mantra "keep things simple" is helpful with regard to being happy. Otherwise, it's easy to feel overworked, oversubscribed, overly stressed, and overwhelmed – all of which lead in the opposite direction of happiness.

There's probably something going on in your life now that is difficult, stressful, or discouraging. Think about it from a different vantage point. Take action to make it feel less complex and less confusing. Ask yourself, "How can I turn this situation into a Brazilian bakery for me?" Wake up and smell the coffee.

I'll Be Happy When...

In *Minding the Body, Mending the Mind*, Joan Borysenko of the Mind/Body Clinic at Harvard Medical school, wrote:

> How many times has your mind told you that you could be happy if you lost ten pounds? Made more money? Then, even if these things come to pass, you just move on to the next set of conditions for happiness. The conditions are like the proverbial carrot that dangles in front of the donkey. You never reach them... Deferring happiness until any condition is met – a new job, a new relationship, a new possession – leads to suffering.

Are you postponing your happiness? When you place conditions on your happiness, it is like not allowing yourself to be happy now. The conditional happiness notion doesn't really work. You'll just want more, bigger, better, and different in a never ending fashion. If you thought a salary of $50,000 would bring you contentment, you might be a bit surprised when you get there that you start thinking about $75,000 so quickly. That three bedroom home you were certain would satisfy you somehow doesn't do the trick anymore. But you're certain the new house or the renovation will make you happy. We find ways to not allow ourselves to be happy with our current set of circumstances. We place conditions on our happiness, the effect being we don't give ourselves permission to be happy here and now.

In *No Death, No Fear*, Thich Nhat Hanh, the prolific Vietnamese author and teacher suggests the importance of recognizing that the conditions of happiness that are already there in your life are enough. This recognition can bring immediate happiness because you have now stopped craving for more and have no need to postpone happiness. You have given yourself permission to be happy. Barry Neil Kaufman heartily agrees with Thich Nhat Hanh.

In his book, *Happiness Is a Choice*, Kaufman states, "Although we have grown accustomed to creating happiness in response to favorable events or interactions, no stimulus is actually required." That is quite interesting. In other words, he's telling you that happiness is a choice, and that you can make that choice right now. It seems that misery is optional, not inevitable, and that it at least partially follows the unnecessary conditions you may place on your happiness. He urges you to make the "decision to be happy" by making the decision to stop being unhappy.

So, I would recommend that you develop an awareness of what conditions you place on your happiness. Don't tell yourself, "I won't be happy until I _____." If you're busy waiting for certain conditions to occur for you to be happy, it's possible you may have a long wait. It's okay to be happy now.

If you want to be happy, be.
-Henry David Thoreau

Most folks are about as happy
as they make up their minds to be.
-Abraham Lincoln

The Whole Truth and Nothing But the Truth

When I taught a college course in general psychology, I enlisted the help of two students to aid me in doing an experiment. Unbeknownst to the other students in the class, I asked the two students to start a fight (verbal and physical) in the front of the classroom shortly before I was to arrive. They were given exact instructions as to how to stage it, including who said what and who did what. After the fight was to begin, I'd enter the room and break it up. We rehearsed it several times, sticking to the script verbatim. The day of the "fight" came and went according to plan. They fought. I broke it up. I sent them to the Dean's office.

I asked each class member to write a few paragraphs about what happened. I asked them to include details such as who started it, who threw the first punch, and specific comments they remembered. The reports were markedly contradictory. Despite witnessing the same event, the details were reported vastly different. It turned out to be a draw. Half the class had one student as the first puncher, while the remaining half went with the other student. What people thought they saw and heard did not necessarily match with what actually transpired. These people writing the reports were not lying. They strongly believed in their versions of the events. They'd swear by their vivid recollections that what they wrote was the truth.

Most of them were astounded when we played back a recorded tape (I had a third student unobtrusively record the entire staged fight from the rear of the classroom). I was not surprised at all. Numerous social psychology experiments have validated that people's ego functions, including memory, are significantly influenced and distorted by their own feelings, needs, and idiosyncratic perceptual filters. People see what they want and hear what they want. Thus, the infamous "he said/she said" dynamic. I've worked with countless couples who recount an argument they've had in which each person recalls totally different words that were uttered.

One of them says something, and the other hears something that may bear little resemblance to what was actually said. Or, the person who actually said the words no longer remembers saying those exact words. Defensive mechanisms are at work.

It's hard to get people to believe that they may have distorted the events and words they purported to see and hear. They have no problem believing someone else could be an inaccurate or biased reporter, but most people are unwilling to even entertain the idea that it could apply to themselves. There is a phenomenon that is widely accepted in the field of psychology that is called the "better than average" effect. Studies conclude that people judge themselves as being better than the average person on just about every possible dimension. This perceptual bias leads to unhappiness. In one study where individuals were asked to rate themselves on 40 character traits in comparison to the average person, most people rated themselves more positively than average on 38 of the 40 traits. In other words, they saw themselves as being better than the average person on traits such as friendliness, intelligence, maturity, dependability, kindness, sense of humor. The overwhelming majority of people rate themselves as being more ethical than others and as being better drivers and better lovers. They also believe they are less prejudiced and less mean, and that they are more likely to go to heaven.

All of these assumptions create possible interpersonal problems. People think they know best. They think their version of events is much more accurate than anybody else's. Therefore, they truly believe other people's interpretations of events are wrong. Thus, they overestimate what they believe people can learn from them and they underestimate what they can learn from others. Most people therefore are better at giving advice than accepting it.

To be happier, it would be helpful to accept that you don't have the market cornered when it comes to truth or accuracy. Don't quickly discount other people's accounts by telling yourself what really happened or what was truly said. Keep in mind that you may be seeing the world a bit askew as you see it through your own set of lenses that have been created by your history and needs. Try to remember that truth may not always be exactly as you experience it. Being less defensive will lead to less conflict, less anger, and fewer power struggles.

A man entered the woods and saw a chameleon on a tree. He reported to his friends, "I have seen a red lizard." He was firmly convinced that it was nothing but red.

Another person, after visiting the tree, said, "I have seen a green lizard." He was firmly convinced that it was nothing but green.

But the man who lived under the tree said, "What both of you have said is true. But the fact is that the creature is sometimes red, sometimes green, sometimes yellow, and sometimes has no color at all.

-*The Power of Myth* by Joseph Campbell

My friend Joey continues to remind me that, "There is no such thing as the truth, there are only stories."

Do the Right Thing

Johann Wolfgang Van Goethe once said, "Let everyone sweep in front of his own door and the whole world will be clean." The Dalai Lama has a different way of getting at this. Before making any decision, he suggests you ask yourself the question, "Will it bring me happiness?" If you are pondering whether to have the affair, eat the cheesecake, go to the party, gamble, take the drug, exercise, watch television, or volunteer, asking yourself that question may help you to pause, reflect, and decide upon actions that help you to create your happiness. Asking yourself the question will help you to discern the differences between fleeting pleasure and lasting happiness.

If and when you reach old age, whether you have integrity or are despairing will depend on how you've lived your life and the choices you made. You know what they say about pregnancy. You can't be a little pregnant. You're either pregnant or you're not. It's like that with integrity. Either you have it or you don't. Mother Teresa has said, "Do not wait for leaders. Do it alone, person to person."

Word spread across the countryside about the wise Holy Man who lived in a small house atop the mountain. A man from the village decided to make the long and difficult journey to visit him. When he arrived at the house, he saw an old servant inside who greeted him at the door. "I would like to see the wise Holy Man," he said to the servant. The servant smiled and led him inside. As they walked through the house, the man from the village looked eagerly around the house, anticipating his encounter with the Holy Man. Before he knew it, he had been led to the back door and escorted outside. He stopped and turned to the servant and said, "But I want to see the Holy Man!"

"You already have," said the old man. "Everyone you may meet in life, even if they appear plain and insignificant...see each of them as a wise Holy Man. If you do this, then whatever problem you brought here today will be solved."

Henry James said, "It's time to start living the life you've imagined." For happiness and peace of mind, your actions need to be in harmony with your thoughts. It's not enough to think about doing the right thing or knowing what the right thing to do is. It's vital that you do the right thing. J.C. Watts said, "Character is doing the right thing when nobody's looking."

What do you think gives life it's purpose and meaning? It may be a valuable question for you to come to terms with. Your answer may provide a road map for you as you seek to be happier. Why? If you are leading a purposeful and meaningful life, the likelihood of your being happy is vastly higher than if you are not leading such a life. I find purpose and meaning in being a useful and responsible person who honors commitments, works and plays hard, loves deeply, and who believes in the importance of acting compassionately. Above all, I try to do no harm and manifest a generosity of spirit. This gives me that road map to happiness.

What does doing the right thing mean to you? Do you have a roadmap that works for you? Is your map leading you in the direction of integrity? Integrity is one of those core character traits that self-actualized people seem to possess. Being honest, being responsible, and being able to look at yourself in the mirror all increase the likelihood that you'll be happier. If you haven't done the right thing, strongly consider doing the next right thing. Your self-respect will grow in relation to your doing the right thing.

It may be tempting to go in other directions. I'd urge you to be skeptical of shortcuts. Read the fine print. If it sounds too good to be true, it probably is. Most places worth getting to require time, effort, and patience. It is anything but easy to continually work on doing what's right. It might be easier to rationalize, suppress, deny, and continue to deceive ourselves, when beneath it all we know that we didn't quite step up to the plate and do what we needed to.

The Eskimo hunter asked the missionary,
"If I did not know about God and sin, would I still go to hell?"
"No," said the missionary, "not if you did not know."
"Then why did you tell me?" asked the Eskimo.
-After the Ecstasy, The Laundry

Don't Blink

Last night was a bit of a landmark for me. I got into the movies for the senior citizen price. First time. It was a funny feeling. I saved $2.50 at the cost of seeing myself from a different perspective. Ambivalence. I'm trying to digest the experience. Does this mean I'm beginning the end stage of my life? Am I old? Two of my brothers and my father all died at about age 71. Does this mean I've got ten years left at best? You know how quickly ten years fly by. Gee, maybe I should have just paid the regular price of admission. But, even if I did, does that really change anything? It's like holding your stomach in when you're getting weighed.

The good news is that I don't feel old and that I've always had an appreciation of the passage of time with respect to how to live my life. I frequently remind myself to look over my left shoulder. That's what Don Juan, the Yaqui Indian Sorcerer, instructed Carlos Casteneda to do. He told him that if he looks in that direction, he'll be able to catch a glimpse of his death stalking him. He urged Carlos to see his impending death as an honest advisor who would help him gain perspective on what matters and what he should do. He urged Carlos to not waste time and reminded him not to spend his time being worrisome, unhappy, or regretful. I enjoy a lot of leisure activities and when I pursue them, I don't feel as if I'm wasting time. I never "kill time." I have more of a sense of respect for time and how I want to use mine.

The thought fleetingly crosses my mind that I better write this book as fast as I can. Neurons are kicking the bucket as I write this sentence. Will my creativity, lucidity, and intelligence erode with each passing month? Being the eternal optimist, I shift gears and decide to invest myself in the belief that I still have a few more good books in me. But, I decide to write as fast as I can anyhow. I'm optimistic but not naïve. I know anything can happen at any time. That's the part of the bargain that life brings. I accept it.

So I'm officially a senior citizen. I'm already starting to see that it's just a label, nothing I have to define myself as. Age is just a number. We all know old forty year olds and young eighty year olds. We're all older than we were yesterday. I'm grateful that I'm getting older. I prefer that to the alternative. Studies on happiness point to what is termed "transcendence" as being a virtue related to life satisfaction. Transcendence is comprised of the character strengths of gratitude, hope, humor, appreciation of beauty, and spirituality. Developing these character traits helps to transcend issues regarding aging.

I'm going to take it day by day, doing the things that feel right. I'll run as long as I can as long as I can as long as I can. I'll treat myself, my family, and others well. I'll take chances, make mistakes, keep an open mind, and redefine 60, 70, 80...(hopefully). And, I'll look forward to getting $2.50 off on the price of admission.

Salad Days

You can get used to just about anything. This is not necessarily a good thing. My friend Tony tells the story of the first day he was stationed in Vietnam. He needed to move his bowels. It was about 100 sultry degrees as he walked toward the bathroom. Make that the latrine. Make that large outhouse. He opened the door and entered. He just about got sick to his stomach. The stench was pervasive. It was difficult to breathe. There were flies everywhere. Bugs of various shapes and sizes lined the floors and walls. The thought ran through Tony's mind, "This place is a shithouse!" It was hard to put anything over on Tony. The "toilets" were like long boards that had half-a-dozen holes where people could sit. Miracle of miracles, Tony no longer felt the urge to go to the bathroom.

Fast forward one month. Tony is relaxed and humming while thumbing through a couple of magazines. And yes, this is happening while he is sitting in the same outhouse described above. When we need to adapt, we do. In fact, Tony is in no hurry to get out of there. And, remember that horrendous smell. It's now, "What smell?" The flies and bugs are just sharing space with him as Tony and his "neighbors" share jokes and stories.

The obstacle is the path.
-Zen Proverb

As we age and accumulate life experiences and maturity, we realize the need to make accommodations. Idealism and the wish for Utopian-like existence are replaced by realism and a wish for relative health and well-being. The term "salad days" was coined by Shakespeare in "Antony and Cleopatra," and referred to a time of youthful inexperience and innocence, the best time of youth. In high school and college, Tony thought his salad days might last forever. Then came Vietnam. Tony came to understand he needed to let go of his picture of what "ought to be" and make peace with things as they actually were. Paraphrasing Dr. Dan Baker, "You can wrestle with God – but it's a fight you never win."

At the outset, I said we can get used to just about anything, but that is not necessarily a good thing. Don't get used to anything that puts you in harm's way. Don't get used to anything illegal, unethical, immoral, or that just doesn't feel right to you. Don't adapt to self-destructive habits or relationships. In those instances, not adapting will increase your self-respect and give you a chance to be happier.

Keep It Simple

Many people are experts at complicating their lives. They continually struggle with physical and mental exhaustion. They over-think rather than cutting to the chase. They create catch 22's. In Joseph Heller's novel *Catch 22*, Yossarian doesn't want to be a pilot anymore but the only way he can get out of flying is to be declared insane. The catch is that if he recognizes that he's insane and asks not to fly, that is proof of his sanity. I've worked with lots of brilliant and creative people who generate vast amounts of thoughts, most of which complicate their lives. My guess is that it would behoove you to make an effort in the direction of learning to simplify. Catch yourself in the act of over-thinking and put up a stop sign (visualize the red octagon shaped sign) and tell yourself, "There I go again." Over-thinking leads to fear and worry. It isn't necessary to understand every ramification of every possibility that exists with regard to what you're thinking about. Over-thinking is a futile attempt to control everything.

Another way people complicate their lives is by being over-subscribed with regard to magazines. As the magazines and books accumulate, we're faced with an ever growing pile of unread material that contributes to our feeling frustrated and under the gun, so to speak. But this over-subscription extends far beyond magazines. People routinely tell me that they have no time for themselves; that they wish they had time to work out or get a massage, but that they don't. It might be that between working and taking care of the kids and everyone else, they feel like there's no time left for them.

Wait a second. Who's running the show? This is your life. If you have no time for yourself, perhaps you should consider making it a bit simpler. Easier said than done? I have empathy for your plight, but more or less, we're all in the same boat. Dr. Thomas Arnold Bennett offers his take on it:

> You wake up in the morning and your purse is magically filled with 24 hours of un-manufactured tissue

of the universe of your life! It is yours. It is the most precious of possessions. No one can take it from you. And no one receives either more or less than you receive.

If you are always hurrying and scurrying and feel exhausted and as though you have no time to get to the things you'd like to do, it may be time to simplify. If it's all too complicated and overwhelming, you need to come up with a new happiness equation.

People are always blaming their circumstances for what they are. I don't believe in circumstances. The people who get on in this world are the people who get up and look for the circumstances they want, and, if they can't find them, make them.
-George Bernard Shaw

Start by slowing down and giving yourself some time and space to get more balance in your life. You may need to resign from something, delegate certain responsibilities, or enlist some help. The aim is to restore a non-complicated, simple way of thinking and acting that produces satisfaction rather than a sense of being overburdened and having no time for yourself. We all have the same basic needs to satisfy. We all have the same 24 hours each day. Become a simplifier, not a complicator.

The old man, believing in the axiom that it's never too late to learn, decided to take piano lessons. He went to see a teacher and inquired about the cost. "Twenty dollars for the first lesson, ten dollars for subsequent ones," said the teacher.

"Excellent," said the old man, "I'll start with the second lesson."

How Can I Help?

Makenzie Snyder has been helping foster children since she was seven years old. That's when she learned that many foster children have nothing but a plastic garbage bag to carry their belongings to temporary homes. Makenzie felt strongly that she wanted to help, so she began collecting duffel bags and stuffed animals, which would be distributed to foster children via social workers. She thought about how she loves to cuddle with a stuffed animal when she feels sad or lonely, or when her family is away on a trip. So it was that she began shopping at yard sales for the needed items. Then, she got backing from a foundation and began getting financial contributions. In the past seven years (she's 14 now), Makenzie has supplied duffel bags and stuffed animals to well over 30,000 children. There are over a half-million foster children in the United States, and she hopes to eventually get to them all.

> Life's most urgent question is
> what are you doing for others?
> -Martin Luther King, Jr.

Craig very much admired his father who was in his 80's. His father was a well-respected pillar of the community who reached old age with integrity and peace of mind. Craig felt that his father was a very happy man. He told me that his father's credo for as long as he could remember was, "How can I help?" That was the type of guy that he was. A mensch. A real human-being. Wow, think how powerful those words are and what a difference they can make. There's an old saying to the effect that when two Jews meet, if one has a problem, the other automatically becomes a rabbi. I think Craig's father was that kind of man.

If you are less than happy, helping others is the best medicine for you. Alfred Adler, the famous Neo-Freudian therapist, would advise all of his depressed patients to do nice things for others.

That was their assignment. In doing so, they became less preoccupied with themselves while engaging in behaviors that brought benefits to others and themselves.

> There is no exercise better for the heart
> than reaching down and lifting people up.
> -John Andrew Holmes

Dean Sluyter relates an interesting story dealing with sought after spiritual experiences such as reaching satori or nirvana: "One of my teachers tells a story about the time when, as a young seeker in Nepal, he started having intensely blissful meditative experiences and thought they must indicate some kind of momentous spiritual progress. He sat down with his teacher, a seasoned old Tibetan lama, and began to describe the experiences. The lama cut him off with a single question: 'Have they increased your compassion for all beings?' Well, no, they hadn't. 'Then they don't mean a thing.'"

Is helping others really so vital? Yes. No doubt about it. Can your helping others change your life, change the world? Just imagine if everyone believed that life's most urgent question is what are you doing for others.

Andre Schwarz-Bart, in "The Last of the Just," tells of the belief that there are, at all times, thirty-six hidden Just Men (not a politically correct term but I'll use it) upon whom the continued existence of the world depends. They are like secret saints. They're indistinguishable from other human beings and can appear in unrecognizable forms. What separates them from others is the depth of their caring. When one of them dies, another takes his or her place. And, only so long as the Just Men exist, only so long as their special caring continues, just so long will God allow the world to exist. And with each act of special caring by one of the Just Men, God sets forward the clock of the Last Judgment by one minute.

If you want an answer to the question, "How can I be happier?" ask yourself the question, "How can I help?" Consider the old Chinese adage:

> If you want happiness for a year, inherit a fortune.
> If you want happiness for a lifetime, help others.

It Ain't Over 'Til It's Over

The legend of the Maize God holds a prominent place in the culture of the Maya, in which many gods were thought to inhabit the sky, earth, and underworld. The Maize God was lured to the underworld where he was then murdered by the death gods. They buried his body and put his head in a calabash tree. It was seemingly a brutal end to the life of the Maize God. However, that is not the end of the story.

The Maize God had twin sons who were half human and half divine. They boldly entered the underworld and defeated the gods. They resurrected their father. It is no coincidence that the myth of the Maize God has a parallel with the life cycle of corn, which in a sense, is decapitated and reborn each year.

Needless to say, life is filled with challenges to our health, happiness, and survival. I began to see Mary about a year following her "routine" knee surgery. She had been a competent registered nurse at a prominent New York City hospital. She was well-liked by the physicians and other nurses. Something went awry during and after Mary's surgery. She developed an infection following the knee operation. Instead of her leg feeling and functioning better, as she had anticipated prior to the surgery, Mary's leg and pain and mobility got progressively worse. She was left with an abnormal appearing knee, a limp, and a cane. When her condition affected her ability to perform her job, she was promptly let go. Suffice it to say that the surgery was botched and her career screamed to a halt in mid-life.

When Mary came to my office, she was in the midst of a major depression. She felt useless and believed she was a burden to her husband and family. She felt hopeless. Because she was involved in a malpractice case, it was difficult for her to find doctors interested in caring for her. As soon as they heard who the doctor was and which hospital she was suing, consulting physicians were eager to refer her elsewhere. One doctor strongly advised her to seek treatment out of the metropolitan tri-state area (NY, NJ, CT).

Mary was unable to do so many things she had taken for granted prior to her surgery. She couldn't do her nursing job. She couldn't lift her young grandchildren. She couldn't get up and go the way she used to. In effect, she presented me with a laundry list of what she could no longer do. Mary was suicidal. In many ways she was already dead. Her suicide would only serve to make a physiological fact out of what already was a psychological fact. I thought about the Maize God and how he was rescued from death by his twin sons venturing into the underworld. I make my living by going into the underworld. When I'm there, I realize that I am on sacred ground and I typically tiptoe rather than trample. Because my sense of Mary was that she indeed was close to suicide, I decided to forego the tiptoeing. I told her the following story:

In a far off land, two people were taken captive. Each was thrown into a deep well. The wells were side by side. The captors began to shovel dirt into each well. A shovel-full into the first well. A shovel-full into the other. One after another, again and again. Horrible screams emanated from the person in the first well. Barely a sound came from the person in the other well.

The shovelers chatted nonchalantly, paying little attention to either the screaming or the lack of it. An hour passed by before they looked into the wells. One well was completely covered in dirt, having totally buried the screaming person that occupied it. They were astonished when they looked into the other well. Along the edge of the well, there was a series of small steps from the bottom of the well to the top. The person in that well did something amazing. With each shovel of dirt that hit her back, she'd shake it off and pack it together in the form of a small step on the side of the well. With each pile of dirt shoveled upon her, she continued to shake it off and take another small step up – toward the light. She escaped. She never gave up. She was free.

I asked Mary, "Which person are you going to be? The person in the first well or the second?"

As months followed, Mary understood that if her happiness depended on once again becoming the old Mary, she was in trouble. Instead of thinking about everything she could no longer do, Mary needed to discover all the things that she could do, many of which she had never done before. She had to become the new and different Mary, the Maize God resurrected. She needed to explore, take risks, and give herself the opportunity to be born anew.

Maya society documents that dwarves and hunchbacks served to help the Maize God. Teachers come in many different forms and in unusual places. And so it was with Mary's resurrection. People with a variety of challenges and disabilities presented themselves to her when she got the courage to participate in a pool therapy course at a local "Y." Then, one of her neighbors called her for help. The neighbor's husband had taken ill. She called Mary because she knew of her nursing background. Almost instinctively, Mary took charge. She instructed the neighbor to call 9-1-1 while she made her way to the neighbor's house. It was the fastest she had moved since her surgery. She administered the appropriate procedures, identified herself as a nurse, and offered instructions to the police and emergency workers.

Long story short, her actions saved his life. She breathed life into him and herself. She saved his life as well as her own. So, the woman who months earlier felt useless, helpless, and hopeless, grew into her new identity of feeling that she mattered and had plenty to look forward to.

The pain is not so much in the letting go as it is in the holding on. If you want to be happy, stop holding on to who you were or an image of who you think you should be. Get more interested in becoming who you are and who you're capable of being.

The fat lady hasn't sung yet, and Mary and I both heartily agree with that wise old sage, Yogi Berra, who voiced one of the eternal truths forever and ever, "It ain't over 'til it's over!"

Get Ready

It was my fifth year of coaching these kids. They had never won a championship, but were always plugging away. Over the years, we had lost a lot of exciting basketball games by a couple of points. They were fourth graders when we began and were now eighth graders, almost young men. We were playing in a tournament and had made it to the championship game. The trophies to be awarded to each player on the winning team were enormous. All the kids eyeballed them and poked each other in the ribs while uttering exclamations of awe. Let the games begin.

As we stared at the scoreboard after the third quarter, it was hard to believe that we were ahead by fifteen points. In seven minutes, we could be kings of the world, champions, the best. There was a packed house watching. As I looked into the crowd, I saw parents giving me the thumbs up sign. I wanted everyone to be part of this jubilant event. So, I put in the five kids who'd seen the least amount of playing time during the season. You know who I mean. The perpetual bench-dwelling, substitute second stringers. The first team sat down. Not particularly pleased, I might add. The final quarter was quite an event. Remember that fifteen point lead? Well, after four and a half minutes, we were losing by five points. Yes, there was a twenty point swing in four and a half minutes.

We had two and a half minutes left in the game. During a time out, we re-grouped, re-focused, and calmed down. Well, we fought back and found ourselves down by one point with seven seconds to go. We called time out and mapped out a play in which our best shooter would take the last shot. Play began. As the ball was being in-bounded, it was deflected and wound up in the hands of Jimmy, one of our players who had hardly scored a basket the entire season. The clock said three seconds as he took two dribbles toward the foul line area and shot the ball. It was as if time stood still. Those last couple of seconds seemed like an eternity. The noise in the gym seemed to give way to silence. The ball appeared to be moving in slow motion. The buzzer sounded to end the game. If the ball goes in, we win. If it misses, we lose. The ball hit the rim and bounced straight up. It came down, hit the rim again, rolled around the basket, and fell through. We won. Jimmy was a hero and the team carried him on their shoulders. I know it's a moment he'll never forget.

Many years later, I wonder what the consequences would have been if Jimmy's shot didn't go in. I guess, neither Jimmy nor our team would have had that night of glory. But, we still would have gone out for ice cream after the game and still would have had a year-end party. And, if I remember, those second place trophies weren't too shabby. I still would've told the kids I was proud of them and that they should be proud of themselves too. All in all, I don't think any of them would be considerably unhappier now if they had lost then. It seemed to matter a great deal back then, but time has a way of giving a different perspective.

Anyhow, I'm glad we won. Jimmy will tell his grandchildren about it. The shot he was never supposed to take made all the difference. You will get a chance to make a difference. Your efforts and decisions and actions count. You will have an opportunity to make an impact. Be ready for it. See it for what it is. There's the old story of the peasant looking all over the place for his horse while he's riding it. Keep your eyes wide open, your chin up, and get ready. And when the time comes, go for it.

Timing has a lot to do with the outcome of a rain dance.
-An Old Cowboy's Advice

A Tale of Two Vases

My best guess is that it is a random universe. Bad things happen to good people. Good things happen to bad people. Good things happen to good people. All these things occur without rhyme or reason. Life happens. The universe is as it is and won't unfold according to your expectations or wishes. Or mine either.

Glancing at the obituaries in today's Cape Cod Times, the random universe was again manifested. A woman died at 104. Another at 103. A man at 52 and another at 41. It's a pretty similar story, everyday. Everything in its own time. No one wants to go young, but you just never know. Wealth is no guarantee of anything. A Yiddish proverb has it that if the rich could hire people to die for them, the poor could make a nice living.

I think you could probably make a good case for it being an ordered universe. At least it seems to appear that way at times. We have the order of sunrises and sunsets and the seasons of the year. Things seem to make sense at times.

> At high tide, fish eat ants.
> At low tide, ants eat fish.
> -Thai Proverb

But, I still lean toward the "you never know what you're going to get" ideology, and you may never fully know why. It's not necessary for you to know all the details of why things happen. It is helpful if you understand you can't truly control life, even if you develop obsessive compulsive rituals or routines. What you can get better at controlling are your reactions to events. The following story was printed in my book, *Seven Times Down, Eight Times Up: Landing On Your Feet In An Upside Down World*. So many people told me how important the story was for them, so I've decided to present it again.

There is a Taoist story of a farmer whose horse ran away. That evening his neighbors gathered at his farmhouse to offer their condolences on his bad luck. He said, "May be." The following day, the horse returned and brought with it six wild horses. All the neighbors came by to congratulate the farmer on his good fortune. He said, "May be."

The next morning his sixteen year-old son tried to ride one of the wild horses. He was thrown and broke his leg. Again the neighbors came to offer their sympathy for his misfortune. The farmer said, "May be." The following afternoon, army officers came to the village to seize young men to fight in an unjust war. The farmer's son was rejected because of his broken leg. When the neighbors came in to say how fortunate everything had turned out, the farmer said, "May be."

I believe your happiness level is directly related to your acceptance of the randomness of the universe. If you take it personally, you may think, "Why me?" and may feel like a victim. Things are as they are.

Katie Lynch is twenty eight inches tall. Leonid Stadnik is eight feet four inches tall and is still growing.

As you may know by now, I was the youngest of six children of hard-working but fairly poor parents. We always lived in small apartments. My sibs and I played sports in the living room because it was the only room of size in the apartment. Mom and dad were at work and we were pretty much unsupervised. We played basketball, football, wiffleball, and just about every other kind of ball in that room. Over the years, we managed to break 90 percent of the inexpensive artifacts, make that chochkas, on display in the living room. And, we moved at least 13 times that I can remember. One object survived intact. My brother, sister and I still talk about it, and we believe it's at least 60 years old. It's an odd looking, rather ugly vase with Greek mythological figures on it (Pan and Nymphs). The family vase that was right in the middle of all the action for decades remains unscathed, despite all the ball playing, all the wrestling matches, and all the moves that occurred. After my parents died, the vase went to my brother Sam. Shortly before he died, he and his wife told me they wanted me to have it. This cheap, ugly family vase now is proudly displayed in my dining room. My wife, Nan, was equally honored to have it.

In his book, *Who Dies?*, Stephen Levine tells the following story that I have taken the liberty of modifying slightly:

Once someone asked a well-known Thai meditation master, "In this world where everything changes, where nothing remains the same, where loss and grief are inherent in our very coming into existence, how can there be any happiness? How can we find security when we see that we can't count on anything being the way we want it to be?"

The teacher, looking compassionately at this fellow, held up a gorgeous glass vase that had been given to him earlier in the morning and said, "You see this vase? For me, this vase is already broken. I enjoy it. It holds flowers admirably and sometimes reflects the sun in beautiful patterns. If I should tap it, it has a lovely ring to it. But when I put this vase on a table and someone knocks into the table and the vase falls to the ground and shatters, I say, 'Of course.' When I understand that this beautiful new vase is already broken, every moment with it is precious. Every moment is just as it is and nothing need be otherwise."

So, back to the unscathed family vase. I understand it's already broken, as is the newborn, the senior citizen, the new car, my friends and family and myself. That's why I'm happy, and that is why every moment is precious.

The Sound of Music

Deep inside the Brazilian rainforest lives a type of tree found nowhere else in the world. It is Caesalpinia Echinata, more commonly known as the pernambuco tree. This imperiled tree is becoming scarce. There is an organization called the International Pernambuco Conservation Initiative, dedicated to saving the species. There is worldwide concern. The future of music is at stake.

Stringed instruments such as violins, violas, cellos, and basses are dependent on the wood from pernambuco trees, and have been since the time of Mozart. The world's greatest musical artists agree on the necessity to rescue the pernambuco and create conditions for it to thrive. I was shocked when I found out that the actual stringed instruments are not even fashioned from the wood of pernambuco. If the violins are not made from the tree, why would classical music be in jeopardy? Pernambucos are used to make bows. Archetiers are craftsmen who make bows for violins and other stringed instruments. They will tell you that pernambuco wood is the only material out of which a top-quality, high-performance bow can be made. And that includes synthetic or natural materials.

Russ Rymer has written an excellent article called "Saving the Music Tree" that was printed in the *Smithsonian*:

The bow is the Cinderella of the orchestra, the overworked, overshadowed helpmate of its more glamorous partners. Few people, even among lovers of classical music, think of the bow as an instrument in its own right, but players of stringed instruments know better. "Some people think a bow is only wood and hair," says Gunter Seifert, violinist with the Vienna Philharmonic and head of the Wiener Geigen Quartet. "But the bow can be more essential to expressing the soul of the music than the violin is." For this reason, pernambuco bows are used by almost all serious orchestral and chamber musicians, whether they be professionals or amateurs, and by most advancing students, who learn early in their education that "it's better to have a fine bow and a mediocre violin than a fine violin and a mediocre bow."

So the unrecognized bow has a crucial role in producing the music of Beethoven, Bach, Haydn, and Mozart. The pernambuco is the wood used to create the bow that partners with the violin to produce incredible music. The pernambuco is the material of your mind. The bow is your thoughts. Your thoughts partner with your body and behaviors to produce happiness. Just as most people don't recognize the importance of the material of the bow in producing the music, you don't recognize the importance of your thoughts in producing happiness. An inferior bow produces inferior music despite the quality of the violin. Your negative thoughts produce unhappiness despite your attributes, health, wealth, character, and so on.

There are additional parallels between the pernambuco and your mind. Pernambucos have innate characteristics of strength, resiliency, pliability, and lightness. But pernambuco wood can also be thorny and twisted, and only a portion of the wood is suitable for use with regard to the bows that are hand-produced by the archetiers. And you too must be discerning. You must pick and choose from the raw material of your mind. You must discard the unusable (thorny) thoughts that are not suitable for creating happiness, and become a psychological craftsman akin to the archetier. You learn to harvest what produces happiness. It takes years of seasoning for the pernambuco sticks to be able to be shaped and used optimally to produce the sound they are capable of producing. It will also take awhile for you to create the happiness you are capable of experiencing. Remember that organization I mentioned earlier that's dedicated to saving the pernambuco? They're taking action right now but they're in it for the long haul. Start now. Be patient. You are the violinist, the violin, the bow maker, and the bow. Make beautiful music.

Move It

I run a lot. Years ago I ran five years without missing a day. I ran in any kind of weather. Once, the winds of a tropical storm blew me backwards during a run. Looking back, I guess I was running compulsively. Now, I'm more selective. I haven't done a marathon in a few years and typically run about four or five days a week. I'll do 5-K and 10-K road races. For some reason, people seem to have the need to tell me of the dangers of running. Not just that I can get hit by a car, but that it's bad for my bones and my joints, and that the pounding is generally bad for my body. Here's how I look at it: it's much more dangerous to be sedentary.

Lots of people remind me that Jim Fixx died in his early 50's. He was the guy who wrote the classic book *The Complete Book of Running* that helped popularize the running movement starting in the late 1970's. I understand that running doesn't guarantee good health or immortality. Still, I do know that Jim Fixx's father and grandfather both died of a congenital heart disease in their 30's. Jim Fixx's running probably prolonged his life rather than contributed to his demise.

I strongly believe that there are many benefits associated with exercising (not just running). There are obvious physiological benefits such as cardiovascular conditioning, weight control, and reduced risk of hypertension and various other diseases. The psychological benefits are also legion. In fact, there is a wealth of research supporting exercise as an adjunct to treating anxiety and depression. It makes sense. It gets you moving in a forward direction. You're doing something positive for yourself. It's hard to feel depressed while you are intensely exercising. Vigorous exercise produces changes in brain waves and biochemistry. Chemicals are produced that are anti-depressive in nature.

Begin wherever you're at. Don't rush it. Do whatever you can. Each week, add one to two minutes to your routine. For example, if you're walking 12 minutes now, do that three or four times for a week. Then, make it 13 minutes each time you walk the next week. The following week, make it 14 or 15 minutes and so on.

> Grain by grain, a loaf.
> Stone by stone, a castle.
> -Yugoslavian Adage

After a month or so, try picking up the pace a bit. Throw in an occasional hill. You can try mixing brisk walking with short bursts of light running. There are many variations of the theme, but the idea is to find something in the way of exercise that you'll continue so that you can accrue the potential benefits. Vigorous activity is one of the antidotes for unhappiness.

> If you are facing in the right direction,
> all you have to do is keep on walking.
> -Buddhist Proverb

Foofaraw

Stacey lived in an apartment building on the sixth floor. One morning she met up with her neighbor on the way to the elevator. Although they had been friendly neighbors for a couple of years, on this particular morning, it seemed that he had very little interest in chatting with her. He seemed abrupt and aloof. This bothered Stacey more and more as the day went on. She turned it over and over in her mind again and again. What could be wrong? Why was he so cold and distant? Then, it hit her. Aha! She remembered that about a week ago, she had borrowed his hammer and that she still had not returned it. The more she mulled it over, the more furious she became. How dare he be so rude, all because of a cheap hammer. She was incensed. That evening, she got the hammer and knocked on her neighbor's door. When he opened it and said, "Hi Stacey," she replied loudly, "Take your damn hammer, you jerk!"

We can become experts at making the proverbial molehill into the proverbial mountain. And usually we do this for no good reason at all. It's a form of self-torture most likely related to our feeling a bit too insecure about ourselves or a bit too guilty. My guess is that Stacey's neighbor was stunned by the way she returned the hammer and had no idea why she was so upset. As to his apparent lack of response to her near the elevator that morning, it probably had nothing to do with anything related to Stacey. I always remember a line from a hit song (from the 70's I think) that says, "Don't let the sound of your own wheels drive you crazy."

In an interesting book called *The Zen Commandments*, the author addresses how our thinking can undermine life's simplicity. He states, "We can however, make it very complicated. There's no straight line that can't be made crooked, no easy task that can't be made hard, no clear statement that can't be obscured, no ordinary encounter that can't be twisted into ingenious and endless ramifications."

A foofaraw is when a large fuss is made over a matter of little importance. Yes, it's a real word. You can look it up in the dictionary. I'm sure you remember the Y2K thing and how that turned out. People were hoarding water and food, withdrawing lots of cash from the bank, turning cartwheels, juggling, and anticipating various problems of significance. It came and went. Foofaraw. We can create foofaraws daily. We can become experts at it. Your chances of happiness are much better if you get the equivalent of a foofarawectomy.

The greatest discovery of any generation is that human beings
can alter their lives by altering the attitudes of their minds.
-Albert Schweitzer

Junk Mail

Neurosis refers to a condition in which the individual is unhappy and worried much of the time. The great theorist, Alfred Adler, once said that, "Neurosis is largely a matter of attention." Recent studies conducted at the University of Georgia Psychology Department support Adler. The findings show that people with social phobias do not disengage their attention from socially threatening ideas. Rather, they indulge the ideas that point to the likelihood of their being rejected, embarrassed, humiliated, or ignored. Another recent study presented in the international journal *Behavioral Research* and Therapy further confirmed Adler's premise. Research stemming from the Department of Psychology at San Diego State University focused on what highly anxious people attended to. It turned out that the negative meta perceptions of those with social anxiety were more a function of their own self-perceptions than the negative perceptions of others.

A thirsty lion, having found his way to a lake, was startled when he bent over to take a drink, to see another lion looking back at him. He growled at it but it didn't go away. He became consumed by this threatening looking lion and roared at it again and again. Finally, he charged into the lake to attack the "other lion," only to discover that there wasn't any other lion there at all – it was his own reflection.

-Adapted from Idries Shah

When you are feeling unhappy or anxious, remember to ask yourself, "What is it that I've been paying a lot of attention to that's contributing to my feeling this way?" If you were listening to music on the car radio and determined that it was quite grating on your nerves and in fact, was irritating and un-enjoyable, you would change the station. You wouldn't try to bring it in clearer or turn up the volume. You'd simply change the station until you found one that played music more suited for your enjoyment. That's what you need to practice doing with your attention. What you do and do not attend to will definitively influence how you feel. Pay attention to what nourishes you and keeps you hopeful and inspired. Don't cling to or pay undue attention to self-defeating and dispiriting messages. Change the channel.

When junk mail arrives, you don't need to open the envelope and read its contents in order to identify it. It's obvious. There are the bulk mailing rates, advertising propaganda, and the not so unusual address label marked "occupant." Even when they try to personalize it, it's still pretty easy to recognize that it's junk mail. Many of your current thoughts, fears, and worries are the equivalent of junk mail. Get better at recognizing them as such. No need to open them. No need to pay attention to them. No need to save them. You won't need them later. It's just junk.

Give It Away

It's been said that in a Zen temple, there's nothing to steal because everything of value has been given away. Practice giving away yourself. Giving away your love and compassion. Do you tell and show every important friend and family member that you love them? Do you go out of your way for them? Making the extra effort will increase your joy, as well as theirs. The business guru, Jim Rohn, relates the following story:

> When my father was still alive, I used to call him when I traveled. He'd have breakfast most every morning with the farmers...little place called The Decoy Inn out in the country where we lived in southwest Idaho. So Papa would go there and have breakfast and I'd call him just to give him a special day. Now if I was in Israel, I'd have to get up in the middle of the night, but it only took five minutes, ten minutes. So I'd call Papa and they'd bring him the phone. I'd say, 'Papa, I'm in Israel.' He'd say, 'Israel! Son, how are things in Israel?' He'd talk real loud so everybody could hear – 'My son's calling me from Israel.' I'd say, 'Papa, last night they gave me a reception on the rooftop underneath the stars overlooking the Mediterranean.' He'd say, 'Son, a reception on the rooftop underneath the stars overlooking the Mediterranean!' Now everybody knows the story. It only took five to ten minutes, but what a special day for my father, age 93.

Much of the time, it's easy to take family and friends for granted. Don't. These are the people who really know you and amazingly enough, still love and value you. I tell my family members and friends (male and female) that I love them. Not all of them seem comfortable with that. That's okay. I still tell them. If you've ever been in a crisis, you know who's there for you.

When you hug those closest to you, try doing "hugging meditation," which Thich Nhat Hanh recommends. Hug the person three times. The first time, remember that the person you're hugging will someday be dead. The second time, remember that you also will someday not be here – that you will die. With the third hug, realize that you and the person you're hugging are here, right now, together in this moment, and that this moment will never repeat itself.

Give generously of yourself. Don't be on your deathbed filled with regrets, wishing you had lived more and loved more. Give it away now. While you can. It will come back to you many times over. Tell somebody how special he or she is. Do something nice for them. Show them through your actions. Start today.

> To live in this world
> you must be able
> to do three things:
>
> to love what is mortal;
> to hold it
> against your bones knowing
> your own life depends on it;
>
> and, when the time comes to let it go,
> to let it go.
> -Mary Oliver

Give it away. Do it as if your life depends upon it. It does.

The Life of Meaning

In my previous book, I wrote a story called "The Meaning of Life." If we are specifically addressing one of the most effective ways of becoming happier, we have to use a similar but different title, as I have done above. Leading a meaningful life is associated with happiness. Religious beliefs are able to bring inner peace, a sense of well-being, comfort, joy, and happiness. Praying is also highly correlated with feeling less stressed and happier. Religion fosters a sense of purpose and meaningfulness to counteract the existential dread and absurdity that most humans may encounter at some point in their lives. The benefits of religious beliefs hold up regardless of the particular religious affiliation. It's most likely very comforting to feel as if there's a Universal Force larger than oneself. Also, religion contributes to a sense of belongingness, connectedness, and community.

From 2000-2005, hundreds of research articles on the relationship between religion and mental health were published in academic journals. The overwhelming results? If you're religious, you're likely to be less depressed. You're also most likely to be less anxious. Also, you're probably going to cope better with crises and losses. And, even if you get depressed, you'll be less depressed than a nonreligious person.

"Religion" stems from the Latin "religio," which means "to bind together." It links the individual to family, friends, community, clergy, and congregation. There is social as well as spiritual support on many levels. You don't have to dogmatically practice a religious doctrine in a formalized way in order to reap the benefits. Spirituality, friendship, community, and love are available to you regardless of whether you believe or practice the tenets of any particular religion. In fact, a very recent *Newsweek* poll found that there is "not an explosion of people going to church." The same percentage of people attend weekly worship services now as in 1966. People describe themselves as "spiritual" more often than they do as "religious." The poll revealed that as we age, spirituality increases in importance, as we try not just to know about God, but to experience bliss, rapture, ecstasy, and Oneness. We are looking for "transformative experience."

The Dalai Lama points out that his daily prayers are like reminders to practice compassion, express gratitude, and be loving. He sees his prayers as reminders to be patient, tolerant, forgiving, and kind. He prays daily for four hours. So before you tell me you are busy and can't possibly find the time to pray for 5 or 10 minutes, rethink it! If the Dalai Lama, who's one of the busiest people on the planet, finds the time to pray for four hours a day, are you really going to tell me that you can't find the time to do something of vast importance that is highly correlated with finding meaning and purpose and being happy? Perhaps it would be helpful to reexamine your priorities.

It is true that you can work on yourself spiritually without actually praying, but more Americans pray than do not. It is woven into our private and public lives and is practiced by saints, sinners, seers, and scoundrels. In and of itself, it insures nothing. Prayer has existed since humankind first acquired language. Prehistoric cave drawings have been interpreted to be one of the earliest forms of prayer. Prayer seems to be a universal language. Dr. Sam Menahem, in his book *All Your Prayers Are Answered*, speaks to the power of committing yourself to daily prayers that come from the heart and express gratitude. He believes personal healing as well as possible world transformation may be possible through prayer.

We know that you won't find happiness in the mall. You may not find it in the church, temple, mosque, or zendo either, but your chances are a lot better.

A woman was at work when she received a phone call that her daughter was very sick with a fever. She left her work and stopped by the pharmacy to get some medication for her daughter. When she returned to her car, she found that she had locked her keys inside. The woman looked around and found an old coat hanger that had been thrown down on the ground, but realized she didn't know how to use it. So, she bowed her head and asked God to send her some help.

Within five minutes, an old rusty car pulled up, with a dirty, greasy, bearded man who was wearing an old biker skull rag on his head. The woman thought, "This is what you sent to help me?" But, she was desperate, so she was also very thankful.

75

The man got out of his car and asked her if he could help. She said, "Yes, my daughter is very sick. I stopped to get her some medication and I locked my keys in my car. I must get home to her. Please, can you use this hanger to unlock my car?"

He said, "Sure." He walked over to the car, and in less than one minute, the car was opened. She hugged the man and through her tears, she said, "Thank you so much! You are a very nice man."

The man replied, "Lady, I am not a nice man. I just got out of prison today. I was in prison for car theft and have only been out for about an hour."

The woman hugged the man again and with sobbing tears, cried out loud, "Oh, thank you God! You even sent me a professional."

Life Is Strange

Death is troubling for many people, maybe for most people. It may even be a more troubling idea for those who don't believe in any kind of afterlife in any way, shape, or form. I'd like to ask you a question that I believe relates to your happiness. "What do you have to lose by believing there is some kind of life after death?" Instead of believing that there is absolutely nothing after you die, could you entertain the idea of some kind of life in heaven, or an existence on a soul level, or reincarnation? I just think you might be happier if you had something to look forward to rather than nothing.

In my book, *Seven Times Down, Eight Times Up*, there is a story entitled "The Yogi and the Fork Bender," which begins with the following statement: "I would categorize myself as a down to earth guy. I prefer realism to science fiction. I'm not exactly a 'show me, I'm from Missouri' kind of guy, but I'm close." Magic and so-called miracles typically don't impress me. I don't jump on a lot of bandwagons. I don't believe much of anything that I read and, well, you get the idea. All of this is my attempt to influence your perception of me when you read the next page or so. I'm going to tell you why this person with both feet firmly planted on the ground in this life here and now strongly believes in an afterlife. It's not based on my education, my research, or religion. It's based on three experiences that happened to me.

I don't believe that I'm anyone special or that I have powers that anyone else doesn't. I'm just like you. Ordinary people can have extraordinary experiences. Once you have this kind of experience and begin to share it with others, you find out that a lot of people have had these "strange" experiences. But, life is strange. And that's an understatement.

I'm reminded of the story about the man who goes to a movie and sees an old woman and her dog sitting in the front row. The film was both sad and funny. During the sad parts, the dog cried his eyes out. During the funny parts, the dog laughed his head off.

When the movie ended, the man approached the old woman and said, "That's the most amazing thing I've ever seen. Your dog really seemed to enjoy the film."

The old woman turned to the man and said, "Yeah, it is amazing. He hated the book."

It's kind of mind blowing to think that we were born at all. Out of nothingness, we now have you and me and computers, spacecraft, cloning, chocolate, artificial hearts... Is it really such an incredible leap to believe in some kind of afterlife? Consider doing everything you can in this lifetime to help yourself be happy, including the possibility of believing in an afterlife.

It was the spring of 2001. The hospital called at 1:00 in the morning advising us to get there as soon as possible. My mother was close to death. Although I had said my last goodbyes to her a hundred times before, there would be no one hundred and one. When my wife, Nan, and I got to my mother's room, about 15 minutes after the phone call, she was already dead.

Lying in bed that morning following our sleepless night, we heard a shrill whistling sound in our house. It sounded as if it was very close to us. We tried to find where the sound was coming from, but had considerable difficulty identifying the source. Walking room to room, it seemed pervasive and as if it was in whatever room we went into. Putting my hand in my pocket, I discovered my mother's hearing aid. I had forgotten that I had put it in my pocket at the hospital. That old hearing aid would frequently whistle when the battery was too low or the volume turned too high. I opened the little battery door of the hearing aid. The whistling stopped. So, the mystery was solved. Or, had the mystery just begun? I began shaking and my heart pounded when I saw that there wasn't even a battery in the hearing aid. Do you have a plausible explanation? I don't. If you think this all sounds quite hokey, I understand.

A month later, my brother Sam died. Arriving at home after his burial, I walked into my study. A book had somehow fallen from one of the bookshelves and was sitting by itself on the floor. The book was *Jonathan Livingston Seagull*, by Richard Bach. It was open to page 53. I picked it up and read the following:

"We're from your Flock, Jonathan. We are your brothers." The words were strong and calm. "We've come to take you higher, to take you home."

Jonathan tells them, "I can't lift this old body no higher."

"But you can, Jonathan. For you have learned. One school is finished, and the time has come for another to begin."

As it had shined across him all his life, so understanding lighted that moment for Jonathan Seagull. They were right. He could fly higher, and it was time to go home. He gave one last look across the sky, across that magnificent silver land where he had learned so much.

"I'm ready," he said at last.

And Jonathan Livingston Seagull rose with the two star-bright gulls to disappear into a perfect dark sky.

There were well over 500 books on those shelves.

In the summer of 2003, my brother Bruce died. After the funeral, we returned home and settled in for the evening. I opened the bread drawer and saw a piece of paper lying amidst the breads. It had one word on it. It was a note I had written days earlier to remind myself to call my brother. It was one of many notes, papers, and objects lying around the kitchen counter. Somehow, it wound up in the bread drawer, the drawer containing the staff of life. To re-cap, shortly after Bruce's funeral, I came home, opened the drawer, and found the word "Bruce" on a piece of paper in that drawer. Coincidence? Maybe. But let me add that in the 23 years we've lived in this house, we've never found any note or any other non-bread object in that drawer.

So, maybe it's a stretch, but as I said earlier, I'm not the kind of guy prone to otherworldly beliefs, and it takes a lot for me to jump to conclusions. I'm very happy with this life and I'm willing to wait as long as possible to find out what happens when I die, but now, I'm putting my money on some kind of an afterlife. Hey, I believe it and I think it may add a bit to my happiness. It gives me something to look forward to, hopefully in the long run. When I related the aforementioned events to a friend, I asked him why it's so hard for people to believe in the possibility of an afterlife. He matter-of-factly stated, "Hey, in my previous life, I didn't believe in an afterlife either." Studies have confirmed that people with a firm belief in an afterlife of some sort are basically happier than those without such beliefs. We're not necessarily talking about reincarnation. Many people believe in heaven, or the soul continuing to manifest itself in some fashion. Since no one truly knows, I'm going to be optimistic and choose to believe in some kind of afterlife. Won't you join me?

Odysseus, Penelope, and Calypso

There are many religious traditions and philosophical viewpoints that espouse the idea that this world and this life are just stopovers. They share the perspective that there is a better place awaiting us, something like heaven or nirvana, or bliss, or some version of immortality. We've all been raised to believe, "...and they lived happily ever after," (perhaps in the thereafter). If you could be granted access to eternal life in this kind of setting, would you jump at the chance? Would you be willing to leave life as you know it behind you, including the people that matter to you?

In Homer's *Odyssey*, Odysseus is given that chance. An opportunity of a lifetime. Writing in *UU World*, Dr. Linda Hansen, the minister philosopher, presents the predicament Odysseus encountered. The Greeks had been victorious in the Trojan Wars. Odysseus was on the long road home, trying to return to his wife and family. It was to be an arduous and complicated journey. On the way, he encountered the beautiful and most charming goddess Calypso. She found pleasure with Odysseus and they delighted in their lovemaking. Now, here's where the plot thickens dramatically. Calypso offered to make Odysseus a god. That guarantees immortality. He would not age. He would transcend humanity.

Would this offer present a predicament for you? Or, is it as they say, "a no brainer?" Odysseus thought about Penelope, his finite human wife. He thought about his finite human life. Gently, he responded to Calypso's offer:

> Goddess and Queen, do not make this a cause of anger with me. I know the truth of everything you say. I know that my wife Penelope, when a man looks at her, is far beneath you in form and stature; she is a mortal, you are immortal and unaging. Yet, notwithstanding, my desire and my longing day by day is still to reach my own home and to see the day of my return. And if this or that divinity should

shatter my craft on the wine-dark ocean, I will bear
it, and keep a bold heart within me.

Dr. Hansen and the contemporary philosopher, Martha
Nusbaum, have expounded on Odysseus' decision. In choosing to
be a human being rather than a god, Odysseus chooses suffering
and pain, aging, and death. He is choosing mortal life and everything that comes with the territory. He's choosing to experience
fear, illness, aging, loss, and ultimately the death of Penelope or
himself or both. He's signing up for the whole package. Nusbaum
states, "He is choosing, quite simply, what is his: his own history,
the form of human life and the possibilities of excellence, love, and
achievement that inhabit that form." He is choosing finiteness and
human struggles rather than a struggle-free life of immortality.

Nusbaum makes the poignant point of differentiating what
Calypso and Penelope can offer Odysseus. Calypso can offer wonderful lovemaking and eternal life, but no real story. Penelope can
offer Odysseus a story. Their lovemaking includes the stories they
tell each other about their lives. Calypso can offer pleasure, but
with an asterisk so to speak, denoting that something essential is
missing. And, however you define that missing ingredient, without
it, there may not be true happiness. Odysseus decides to forego
being a god, and in choosing a human life and in choosing Penelope, he chooses to give himself the chance to be happy.

Helen and Maya

Helen Keller was blinded and deafened by a childhood ill-ness. Despite neither being able to see or hear, she went on to graduate cum laude from Radcliffe College and went on to distin-guish herself as an author, lecturer, and administrator. She didn't play it safe. In fact, she once said, "Security is mostly a supersti-tion. It does not exist in nature. Avoiding danger is no safer in the long run than outright exposure. Life is either a daring adventure or nothing."

Helen Keller could have made excuses. She didn't. She approached existence the way Maya Angelou advised, urging you to grab life by the lapel and say, "I'm with you kid. Let's go."

Most people don't live their lives according to the ideas es-poused by Keller and Angelou. They opt for erring on the side of safety, even if it's a miserable safety. They believe that security equates with the absence of danger. But the absence of danger in and of itself may not lead to happiness. Not being willing to risk, to face threat, could produce mild depression, existential guilt, and that over cited but often felt phrase "Is that all there is?" Security is less related to the absence of threat and more related to trust and acceptance of the universe, regardless of the threat. Ideally, that security would come not only from believing in a higher force or presence, but also via a belief in yourself. That belief would be that you could cope with whatever circumstances came your way. Hence, the old Iranian expression, "Trust in God, but tie up your camel," or a similar saying, "In a storm, pray to God but row for shore."

One day a man fell quite ill. He went to the hospital and had some tests. After awhile, his doctor came to his room with the results. The doctor looked at the man's chart and shook his head. He said, "Well, it's not good news. I think you have two hours to live." The man was of course in shock but he asked to be alone.

The man prayed to Great Spirit and said he didn't want to die now. Great Spirit said, "Don't worry, you are going to be fine." The man was relieved, of course.

A few minutes later, an oncologist entered the hospital room with a therapy to offer. The man said no, he would be fine. The oncologist reluctantly left. A few more minutes passed and into the room walked a priest. The man said, "Thank you, Father, but I am going to be fine." The priest also left. Some more time passed and the man was visited by an herbalist, a medicine singer, and many other practitioners.

Two hours later, the man was dead. He was in shock. He walked up to Great Spirit and asked what happened. "You said I was going to be fine!'

Great Spirit replied, "Who do you think sent the help?"

Faith is important, but you have to do your part too. Your ability to be happy will be compromised by your unwillingness to grab life by the lapel. Helen Keller was not dealt a good hand, but she played a poor hand extremely well. When opportunity didn't knock for her, she built a door. Take a lesson from Helen and a hint from Maya.

Ho Hum

Are you bored a lot? If so, you're not going to like what I'm about to tell you. It's your fault! People are bored because they make boring choices. There is a Zen proverb that says, "Painted cakes do not satisfy hunger."

The word "boring" comes from the Latin "borinitus," which means "to not act or to stagnate." In this sense, boring equates to passivity or the lack of seeking stimulation. By the way, I just made up that Latin root idea so as to make my point. In reality, I have no idea of the etymological origins of the word boring.

I think I remember someone once proposing that there should be a profession of "idea cataloguer." It would be this person's job to come up with thousands upon thousands of suggestions to make your life more stimulating and fulfilling. In the absence of such a professional, the task becomes your responsibility. It is necessary to ask yourself what you are and are not choosing that contribute to your boredom. As the noted philosopher Jean Paul Sartre has stated, "You are your choices." If you are waiting to be entertained, stimulated, or excited, you may have a long wait. Create your own list of ideas that will add interest, zest, or passion to your life. Ideas that will make you a happier person.

The reason for looking at boredom has to do with the results of studies that focus on happy people and the characteristics they have in common. In particular, these people have been shown to be curious and zestful. They are open minded, eager to learn, and are willing to take risks. These traits are related to producing active and happy people who are rarely, if ever, bored.

Try some new websites. Learn something new. Take a course. Try a new sport. Do a puzzle. Listen to new music or read a new poet. Bake bread. Spend an afternoon at a new museum. Join a club or organization. Take a hike (literally, not figuratively). Make decisions that could help reshape relationships more to your satisfaction.

Alleviating boredom by doing interesting things does not mean skirting responsibilities. Six college kids who felt bored decided to go to a concert instead of showing up for their Friday biology exam. They devised a story about getting a flat tire and therefore missing the test. They asked if they could have a make-up test. The professor arranged for their exam to be taken a few days later. The six students were each placed in different rooms, each with his or her own proctor. Each student received the exam. On the first page of the test were ten multiple choice questions that were worth one point each. When the students finished page one and turned to page two, this is what they read at the top of the page: "For 90 points, who changed the tire and which tire was it?"

I added the above anecdote just to make this story more interesting, and I'm happy that I did. Remember, you are your choices. Happiness has less to do with finding yourself than it does with creating yourself. It is not a boring world. It's a fascinating world. An amazing world. A world waiting to be discovered by you. Learn, go, join, do, try, discover, play, get involved. Feeling bored means you are not harnessing your potentials and passions in your one and possibly only life. Ben Irwin once said that most of us spend our lives as if we have another one in the bank.

By the way, did I mention that the root of "boring" comes from the French word "bourain," which means "to withdraw?" If you're uncertain if that's factual or if I'm only playing with you, look it up. At least you won't be bored.

Off To See the Wizard

I have a habit of which I know not the origin. Whenever my wife and I get into a car to go on a trip, I emphatically say, "We're off to see the wizard!" Neither of us have ever really talked about it. It's just something I do. Nan doesn't seem to mind. I guess we associate wizards with having all the answers. It's funny that I use that expression so regularly, since I don't generally place a lot of stock in wizards and the like. To me, it's more a matter of trusting my own feelings and my own experiences. I'm skeptical of authority.

A certain man lay bedridden with a serious illness, and it appeared that his death was near. In her fear, his wife summoned the local town doctor. The doctor tapped around on the patient and listened for more than half an hour. He checked his pulse, put his head on the man's chest, turned him onto his stomach and then his side and back. He raised the man's legs and body, opened his eyes, and looked in his mouth. Finally, with a great deal of conviction, he said, "My dear woman, unfortunately I must give you sad news. Your husband has been dead for two days."

At this very moment, the ailing man raised his head in shock and whimpered anxiously, "No, my dearest, I am still alive!"

The wife pushed her husband back down onto the pillow with her hand and replied with irritation, "Be quiet! The doctor is an expert. He ought to know!"

In general, people seem very impressed with fame and fortune. If they get near a famous person, you can see the glitter in their eyes. People seem to think their happiness is related to finding answers from celebrities, llamas, yogis, Zen masters, clergy, gurus, and the like. They'll travel to the Himalayas, to the mountain top, to the ends of the earth. They're off to see the wizards. Hey, I like adventure and travel too. I'm curious, and I'm respectful of those in positions of influence, but if something doesn't sit right with me, I can recognize that.

In his recent book *Still Here*, Ram Dass relates a story that his father used to tell him about an old village tailor named Zumbach:

As legend had it, a man in this village succeeded in business and wanted to have a new suit made. He went to Zumbach, the most famous tailor in the land, and had himself measured. When he came back to Zumbach's shop the next week for the final fitting and put on his new suit and stood in front of the mirror, he saw that the right sleeve was two inches longer than the left.

"Er, Zumbach," he said, "there seems to be something wrong here. This sleeve is at least two inches too long."

The tailor, who didn't like backtalk from his customers, puffed himself up and said, "There is nothing wrong with the suit, my good man. Clearly, it's the way you're standing." With that, Zumbach pushed on the man's shoulder until the sleeves were even. But when the customer looked in the mirror, he saw that the fabric at the back of the suit was bunched up behind his neck.

"Please, Zumbach," the poor man said, "my wife hates a suit that bulges in back. Would you mind just taking that out?"

Zumbach snorted indignantly, "I tell you there's nothing wrong with this suit! It must be the way you're standing." Zumbach shoved the man's head forward until the suit seemed to fit him to perfection. After paying the tailor's high price, the man left Zumbach's store in confusion.

Later that day, he was waiting at the bus stop with his shoulders lopsided and his head straining forward, when another fellow took hold of his lapel and said, "What a beautiful suit! I'll bet Zumbach the tailor made that suit for you."

"Why yes," the man said, "but how did you know?"

"Because only a tailor as brilliant as Zumbach could outfit a body as crippled as yours."

Happy, self-actualized people have a sense of reverence and wonderment with regard to our universe and existence. No one has all the answers. We can't know everything. We don't even know what the next hour will bring. As much as we know about ourselves and about life, there will always be much more that is unknown. Ram Das advises us to "rest in the mysterious present and let the future unfold as it will." This echoes the words of Long Chen Pa, a 14th century Tibetan Dzogchen Master:

Since everything is none other than exactly as it is,
one may well just break out in laughter.

So, although I always seem to say, "We're off to see the
wizard!" I'm not expecting to get all the answers. I'm more aligned
with the essence of Rilke:

Be patient with all that is unresolved in your heart,
and try to love the questions themselves.

Thank You

We are a nation obsessed with sensational stories of tragedies, horrors, crimes, violence, and things that go awry or run amuck. They draw our attention. We're bombarded with constant news of what's going wrong: war, terrorism, bombings, natural disasters, corruption, murder, scandals. We can't seem to get enough of these stories that can leave you shaking your head side to side and talking to yourself. It's like being fascinated with a car wreck. Stop rubbernecking. Enough is enough. It's nice to be informed with respect to what's happening in the world, but when you become overly absorbed and consumed, it rapidly hits a point of diminishing returns.

A lot of our time and energy is taken up by this rubbernecking to see what is wrong with ourselves, our relationships, our families, our country, our world. I would like to propose an idea that I think is rare in our society. Let's rubberneck in the opposite direction. Let's learn to go out of our way to think about what's going right. Let's think about and be thankful for all those things we never really stop to think about.

> The reverse side also has a reverse side.
> -Japanese Proverb

For example: I woke up this morning (thank you for another day). I woke up without a headache or a toothache. No stiff neck either (I'm thankful). There was fresh fruit and cereal in the house. The coffee pot worked. The treadmill worked. The shower worked. We weren't out of shampoo or toothpaste or soap.

It's easy to pay attention and become emotionally charged when these things are not there. But, how about the flip side? Noticing and feeling good and expressing gratitude when the normal day-to-day things occur. The car started right away. I didn't get a flat on the way to the office and I didn't lock my keys in the car when I got out (I feel appreciative). I began seeing patients (feeling grateful I'm healthy enough to work all day). The phones were working. The computer was not down. The fax machine was operating. Rubbernecking to see all the things I take for granted and to express my thanks.

This is not a silly activity. What you see and how you feel will depend on what you look for and pay attention to. Noticing what goes right and not obsessively staring at what goes wrong is going to be a strong determinant of how you feel and how much peace of mind you can obtain. With regard to happiness, attitude determines altitude. Try focusing on what goes right and being grateful.

> If the only prayer you ever say
> in your entire life is thank you,
> it will be enough.
> -Meister Eckhart

The One-Minute Happiness Quiz

The following quiz was developed by Ray Sahelian, M.D. Dr. Sahelian is a respected physician and medical writer. His numerous books focus on health and natural supplements. His website is www.raysahelian.com.

Circle a number in each category. The higher, the truer.

1. I have a healthy personality with high self-esteem, strong willpower, and a positive attitude. 1 2 ③ 4 5

2. I feel connected with and have loving relationships with family, pets, friends, spouse, or lover. 1 2 3 4 ⑤

3. Old or new emotional wounds have healed. I harbor no grudges. 1 2 ③ 4 5

4. I have meaningful goals that I'm passionately pursuing. 1 2 3 4 ⑤

5. Work (and/or school) is satisfying. 1 2 3 ④ 5

6. I am financially secure. 1 2 ③ 4 5

7. I have many interests and pleasures. 1 2 3 ④ 5

8. I am physically healthy, I exercise, sleep well, eat well, and have low stress. 1 2 ③ 4 5

9. I enjoy learning and acquiring knowledge. Furthermore, I use my creative talents. 1 2 3 4 ⑤

10. I have a personal truth or belief system that provides a meaning to my life. 1 2 3 4 ⑤

Score: Total _____

Quiz interpretation:

10-15: Double your Prozac dose.

16-25: There's room for improvement.

26-35: Very good. You can learn to be happier.

36-49: Congratulations! Consider writing your own book on happiness.

50: Incredible! Hold on to something. You may be levitating at any moment.

Check Your Software

In *Easier Than You Think*, Richard Carlson queries about the decision you have to make each and every time you wake up – how to approach the day:

> Are we going to feel sorry for ourselves, or are we going to take responsibility for our own happiness? Are we going to look for what's wrong and find it? Or, are we going to look for what's right and find that instead? Will we see the problems or the opportunities? Will we be part of the problem or part of the solution? Will we be judgmental about life or accepting?

Just about every recent article and book published on the subject of happiness agree on one thing: Unhappy people tend to blame others for their unhappiness. Happy people take responsibility for themselves and how they deal with whatever happens in their lives. Optimists take responsibility. Pessimists blame others or feel cursed. They feel like victims and as if they're continually getting a bad deal. Angry and resentful people play the blame game. Grateful people exhibit acceptance and cultivate a this too shall pass philosophy.

Once upon a time, a wise, old woman took a trip to a strange land. She took a donkey, a rooster, and a lamp. She was refused hospitality in the village inns so she slept in the woods. She lit her lamp to study the holy books before going to sleep. A fierce wind knocked her lamp over and broke it. She said, "So be it," and went to sleep. In the darkness, wild animals came along and drove away the rooster. Thieves in the night stole the donkey. She woke in the morning and assessed the situation. She said, "So be it."

The old woman then went back to the village where she was refused lodging. Enemy soldiers had invaded it during the night and killed all the inhabitants. She also learned that these soldiers had traveled through the same part of the woods where she lay asleep. Had her lamp not been broken, she would have been discovered. Had the rooster not been chased, it would have crowed, giving her away. Had the donkey not been stolen, it would have brayed. Once more, the wise, old woman declared, "So be it."

> Faith is the ability not to panic.
> -Author unknown

In *The Happiness Makeover*, M.J. Ryan asks:

> Can you choose to be happy this very minute? With the floor un-mopped, the conflict with your spouse or child unresolved, the big questions of your life unanswered? Without the future guaranteed? That's what life is really calling us to do, because the only day when it's all sewn up is the day of your death. Until then, we're called upon to enjoy the dance with life in all its messiness and incompleteness.

Being perfectionistic and controlling is a ticket straight to unhappiness. It's nice to have high standards, but having to have things be perfect insures continual frustration and disappointment with life, yourself, and others. Forget about Utopia and Shangra La. This is reality. Things spill. Illness occurs. People will say and do things you wish they hadn't said or done.

Don't be a fault finder. Stop blaming anyone and everyone for your plight. Take responsibility and take charge. You are hard wired for happiness, but your software may need changing. Get rid of the poor me, why me, victim software. Replace it with the happiness solution software that is characterized by accentuating the positive, accepting responsibility for your own happiness or misery, and choosing to be happy. Put in that new software now and start every day by making sure your new software is in place. Get with the program!

Please Make Mistakes

A Japanese proverb has it that "even monkeys fall out of trees." Michael Jordan is considered to be the greatest basketball player of all time. He writes, "I've missed more than 9,000 shots in my career. Twenty-six times I've been trusted to take the game winning shot and missed. I've failed over and over and over again in my life...and that is why I succeed." We all make mistakes from time to time. If you're not making mistakes, you're not participating in life to the extent you need to be. If you're not making mistakes, you probably need to attempt more things and try harder. We're not robots or computers. We are fallible, mistake-making humans.

If you err or fail, try not to beat yourself up. Practice self-acceptance and self-compassion. You will need to forgive yourself for your humanity. Treat yourself with kindness. Getting down on yourself is a direct path to unhappiness, loss of self-esteem, and a poor self-image. Forgiving yourself and encouraging yourself will keep you in the arena. Conversely, being too hard on yourself will lead to the feeling of wanting to take your ball and bat and head home. Withdrawal is taking you in the wrong direction. Wayne Gretzky, the Great One, said, "You miss 100% of all the shots you never take." (Sounds a bit like Yogi.)

Try not to equate mistakes with it being the end of the world. It isn't. Cultivate the glass half-full perspective. Churchill saw it clearly:

An optimist sees an opportunity in every calamity;
A pessimist sees a calamity in every opportunity.

Expressing forgiveness and kindness not just to others, but to yourself, is correlated positively with happiness. Give yourself a break. Give yourself the benefit of the doubt. Learn from your mistakes and move on. Don't beat yourself up and don't beat the proverbial dead horse.

Even the best writer has to erase.
-Spanish Proverb

Go Straight Ahead

My brother Rip has been a salesperson for much of his life. When he began many years ago, it wouldn't be unusual for the following scenario to take place: He'd grab his morning coffee and knock on the first door. If he didn't make a sale, he'd reluctantly try another house. If he didn't sell anything in his first three attempts, he would typically end up in a movie theater for the afternoon. Rip didn't make much money but could intelligently discuss just about any movie you were interested in.

After my father convinced him that it was a numbers game in the sense that the salesperson who sells six out of 30 (20% success rate) actually makes more than the salesperson who sells five out of 10 (50% success rate), Rip made great strides in his chosen field. He claims the biggest lessons he has learned are not to be easily discouraged and to keep going straight ahead.

I think these lessons apply not only to sales, but to life in general. Getting discouraged too easily and too often leads to unhappiness. Going straight ahead means not being overly consumed with regrets and disappointments. It is neither being preoccupied with the past or the future. It's alright to take a look backwards or forwards, but don't stare. The here and now is what you need to focus on and think positively about. Your likelihood of happiness increases when you go straight ahead.

Now, my brother trains salespeople. He tries to cultivate traits of confidence, creativity, optimism, and a sense of humor. These are traits that are helpful while dealing with the challenges of sales and life. Rip likes to tell his trainees the following story:

Two shoe salesmen were called in to speak with their boss. She advised them they were going to be reassigned to a small island in the South Pacific. One would take half the island, and the other one would take the other half. They were instructed to send a progress report as soon as possible. The day after they arrived in the South Pacific, their boss received telegrams from each of them.

The first salesman's telegram said, "Coming home tomorrow. No one here wears shoes." The second salesman's telegram read, "I'll be here quite a long time. No one here has shoes."

What, Me Worry?

Years ago, the creative musician, Bobby McFerrin, penned and performed a best-selling song entitled "Don't Worry, Be Happy." That catchy refrain was repeated over and over again throughout the song. "Don't worry, be happy." Simple advice, yet research confirms the inverse relationship between worrying and happiness. As worry increases, peace of mind and happiness decrease. As worry decreases, contentment and happiness increase.

In the year 2050, they will tell the following story:

Once upon a time, in a land where the pace was frenetic and just about everyone owned SUV's, cell phones, and had 181 television channels, and where 493 billion Big Macs were rapidly being devoured while young children felt the pressure of little league games, and older children and their parents fretted SAT scores, there lived a woman named Pauline. She felt a bit overwhelmed, to say the least. Much of the time, Pauline felt as if she was going to pieces, or cracking up, falling apart, or coming apart at the seams. She felt as if she was being held together by paste, scotch tape, paper clips, a few rubber bands, a bungee strap, and a dab of crazy glue. She feared the worst and felt incredibly fragile. Yes, Pauline was a worrier.

In that same land lived a woman named Julia who faced the same situations and predicaments that Pauline faced. Julia did not feel overwhelmed. She was relatively calm and happy. She befriended Pauline. Everyday, she would tell her, "Worry is useless. It doesn't change anything. It is like beating yourself up for no reason. Your mind is like a garden. Whatever you plant there will grow and thrive. If you plant melons, you get melons. If you plant beans, you get beans. If you plant worries, you get worries. Be careful of what you plant." And so it was that little by little, Pauline learned to reconstruct her garden, to cultivate new crops, and, to be nourished by them.

A centipede was strolling along, humming zip-a-dee-doo-da and having a grand time when he encountered an inquisitive ladybug. She queried, "With a hundred legs, how do you know which one goes after which one? It must be quite confusing!" After that, the centipede became preoccupied with that idea and could barely walk.

Despite the phrase "born worrier," worriers are made, not born. It is a style we learn, and is a style we can unlearn. Our happiness depends on it. John Jay Chapman made the following observation:

> People get so in the habit of worry that if you save
> them from drowning and put them on a bank in the
> sun with hot chocolate and muffins, they wonder
> whether they are catching cold.

We are bombarded with messages that we should be worrying. During the Cold War in the early and mid 1950's, we would practice getting under our school desks to protect us in case of bombings. More recently, we've been coaxed to seal off our windows with duct tape to protect ourselves from chemical warfare. The media will overload you with fear if you allow it to happen. Don't believe much of what you hear. Educate yourself and be selective about what you focus on. Learn to trust your own sense of things.

There was a crow that flew endlessly in search of the Great Crow. It was a rather exhausting endeavor. Finally, he came to a small gathering of crows and posed the question, "Do you know where I can find the Great Crow?"

They looked a little puzzled, but smiled gently and responded, "Don't you know? You *are* the Great Crow."

The noted author Carlos Casteneda studied for years with a Yaqui Indian sorcerer who was the antithesis of a worrier. This sorcerer would teach Carlos that when life is passing by as rapidly as it is, that there is no time for worries and regrets, only time for decisions. He told Carlos to make a warrior's decision (decisive and without waffling back and forth). For happiness, be a warrior, not a worrier.

The Tibetan Book of Wolves and Bicycles

Thirty years ago, on a sunny morning in early spring, I set out on a bike trip with my friends Billy and Carl. We were exploring an area of upstate New York including New Paltz and Woodstock. It was to be an all day expedition and we were all feeling good. We were eager to bike, eat, and maybe even find a rare first edition in a tiny, virtually undiscovered bookstore. The sky was a brilliant, deep azure blue with puffy snow white cumulus clouds. We had all biked together before and we were happy to be doing it again. Beautiful day. Close friends. Biking. Life was good.

In the early afternoon, we somehow managed to leave the rural roads and got on a busy highway. Trucks and cars were zooming by us. Billy immediately suggested we get off that road as soon as possible. We were riding single file and came to a long downhill stretch. Feeling my oats, I went into an all out sprint, passing Carl and Billy. Carl yelled for me to tuck in. As I steered and leaned the bike to the right, I misjudged the maneuver due to how fast I was traveling. The bike was going too far right and was heading off the road. I overcompensated by trying to turn left as my bike's front tire went over the lip at the road's edge. In a heartbeat I was thrown off the bike and landed in the middle of the highway. I landed on my head. (Those of you who know me are probably thinking, "Ah-ha, that explains a lot!")

This was before the day of helmet awareness. None of us even owned helmets. At the time of the accident, I was wearing sunglasses and sucking on a Tootsie lollipop. When my helmet-less head and unprotected face hit the road, I had the presence of mind to realize I was lying on a busy highway. As Billy and Carl quickly helped me off the road, I knew I'd survived the accident. My thick moustache was entirely ripped off upon impact with the road. All my teeth were loose, but still in my mouth. My brain seemed to be functioning alright, although my friends at the scene would take issue with this statement. And so it was that the bike trip ended in favor of the hospital.

My face changed shape and colors with each passing day. For a while, I was barely recognizable. I missed 23 days of work. Billy said the number of days I missed matched my IQ. Carl was equally compassionate. My bike was mangled and beyond repair.

I knew the thing I needed to do. I was, after all, a psychologist. I needed to get back on the horse. I knew that I shouldn't let a lot of time go by. I knew that I should buy a new bike and do such in a timely fashion. Would you say 30 years is timely? It wasn't that I felt afraid whenever I thought about biking again. I just didn't really think about it. I probably was frightened to bike again, but used defense mechanisms to not recognize my fear. Denial. Rationalization. I never owned up to my fear.

Fear is the great inhibitor of action and of possibilities. We're afraid of many things aside from physical harm. Usually we fear psychological threats. Symbolic death-like experiences such as being diminished, failing, being rejected, being abandoned or alone. If you narrow your world and limit your participation in events and interactions due to fear, you will not be as happy as you can be. Many people are afraid of change. Others are afraid of things staying the same. A lot of people are simultaneously afraid of change and of things staying the same.

Fear makes the wolf bigger than he is.
-German Proverb

The age old teachings of *The Tibetan Book of the Dead* provide essential wisdom with regard to facing our fears. Although the book deals with a person's experiences shortly after death, the book could easily be referred to as "The Tibetan Book of Life." It teaches how your fears are just projections of your own mind. Literally or figuratively, if you are facing demons and feeling scared of the aforementioned death-like psychological equivalents, it is because you are haunting yourself. The book is subtitled, *The Great Liberation Through Hearing In the Bardo.* The concept of bardo refers to the gap that occurs when we lose our grounding due to a threat. It's based on the period between feeling confused and transforming the confusion into peace of mind. It relates to the period between fearing insanity and feeling sane. It's about the experience between both life and death, and death and rebirth. I'm speaking metaphorically, although *The Tibetan Book of the Dead* suggests a wider depth of dimension.

When you are in a bardo state, if you can identify and label your fears as projections of your own mind, you will understand how you both haunt and frighten yourself. Your fears will begin to dissipate. Your mind will settle. You will feel more empowered and happier.

I'm happy to say that Carl, Billy and I are bike riding again. I did buy a new bike (my present to myself on my 60th birthday). I just finished a 49 miler on the Cape Cod rail trail. So, I faced my fears and got back up on the horse. And yes, I always wear a helmet.

"Come to the edge."
"We can't. We're afraid."
"Come to the edge."
"We can't. We will fail."
"Come to the edge."
And they came.
And he pushed them.
And they flew.
-Guillaume Apollinaire

The Scream

Once upon a time in a small New Jersey town, an event took place that I will never forget. Let me set the stage. My family had gathered at my parents' apartment for a late Sunday morning breakfast. Tables were arranged so that we could all sit in a large circle and eat together. Fourteen of us breaking bread and engaging in lively conversation that never seemed to be lacking when our family got together.

My siblings and I were raised, at best, in a hard-working, upper-lower class environment without hype or pretense. We were latch key kids before there was such a concept. We were street smart and had to learn quickly how to survive. Of all of us, my brother Sam was the wittiest and gruffest. To say he was a real down-to-earth guy would definitely be an understatement. He was the salt of the earth. He said what was on his mind without fear of consequences and he constantly poked fun, provoked, and made every gathering like a party to be remembered. He was quite a character. Cantankerous, crusty, playful, and as the expression goes, he was full of piss 'n vinegar.

My eldest brother Roy was married to Florence, who was somewhat of a sophisticate, having been raised prim and proper as the only child of a wealthy family. You know the old saying about a fish out of water. That's what it was like when Florence got together with our family. It just wasn't a great fit. Anyhow, back to that unforgettable event. All of a sudden, while we're laughing and talking and generally carrying on in the middle of breakfast, Florence lets out a blood curdling scream. All eyes turn upon her. She could hardly form her words as she held her left hand to her upper chest, slightly below her neck, while pointing to Sam with her right hand.

"Did you see him?" she stammered. "Did you see what he did?" She had a horrified expression on her face. We had no idea what was going on. Florence continued, "Did you see what he did? He dunked! He dunked!"

Evidently, Sam had dunked his bagel in his coffee and Florence was absolutely flabbergasted. Without missing a beat, Sam answered her. "That's right Florence. I dunked. And now I'm dunking in your coffee!" And that's exactly what Sam did as he reached across the table and dunked his bagel in her coffee. It was not even hostile. It was just perfect Sam, playful and irreverent and always looking for a punch line. We all roared. To her credit, even Florence had to laugh.

It is very important to develop a sense of humor, to be able to take things less seriously, to be able to laugh at yourself. If you take everything too seriously, you'll create a heaviness of mind, body, and spirit that weighs you down and creates fatigue, worry, listlessness, and unhappiness. Try to see the humor in things. When studies are done to determine the characteristics that are possessed by happy people, having a good sense of humor is always represented on the list of attributes considered essential for happiness. Lighten up a little bit. It will lighten your load.

Life is a game with rule #1 being:
This is no game,
this is serious.
-Alan Watts

Life is too important to be taken seriously.
-Kierkegaard

If I Only Had a Brain...

For decades, the prevailing wisdom has been that the right side of the brain is the seat of emotions, while the left side of the brain is responsible for logic and rational thinking. In other words, happiness would be related to the right side of the brain. It turns out that recent developments in neuroscience, including the invention of Positive Emission Tomography (P.E.T. scanning), have yielded extraordinary findings. Surprise! Experiments confirm that the seat of happiness is in the left side of the brain rather than the right side. So it appears that happiness, or the lack of it, is intimately connected to our thought processes. Thoughts generating fear, anxiety, and depression light up the right side of the brain. Thoughts that are pleasing, comfortable, and inspiring light up the left side of the brain. One of the bottom lines is that there is such a thing as a happy brain, and it's related to how you think about things.

The biggest troublemaker you'll probably ever have to deal with, watches you from the mirror every mornin'.
-An Old Cowboy's Advice

The neurochemistry and biochemistry of happiness are being aggressively studied. Cognition has to do with the thoughts you generate and how you relate to them. Cognition is an activity of the brain. Speaking of cognition in a recent issue of *American Psychologist*, Dr. Oakley Ray of the Departments of Psychology, Psychiatry, and Pharmacology at Vanderbilt University stated:

> ...this activity of the brain is the body's first line of defense against illness, against aging, against death, and for health and well-being.

So, how you think and what you believe may indeed be a matter of life and death. Dr. Richard Davidson of the University of Wisconsin published research in the *Proceedings of the National*

Academy of Sciences that confirms this idea. Peace of mind, optimism, and happiness reduce the risk of diabetes, hypertension, cardiovascular disease, and many other serious illnesses.

> The mind is its own place,
> and in itself,
> can make a Heav'n of Hell,
> a Hell of Heav'n.
> -John Milton, *Paradise Lost*

The Wizard didn't give the Scarecrow anything. The Scarecrow wanted a brain. He already had one. It wasn't a matter of intelligence that would determine his happiness. It was about how to use his brain intelligently. Happiness has little do with an IQ score. The Scarecrow got motivated and he persevered. He found a group that satisfied his need for love and belongingness. He got inspired and hopeful. He faced challenges and was honest, kind, loving, and courageous. He helped Dorothy, the Lion, and the Tin Man. They, in turn, helped him. He had faith. He was grateful. He finished what he started. In essence, his lament of "If I only had a brain" lead him on a journey of changing how he thought and felt about himself and the world. The Scarecrow changed his thoughts and created a happy brain.

Let's take a minute to review what we know. The left side of the brain (prefrontal cortex) is associated with both logic and happiness. P.E.T. scans reveal that thinking positively lights up the left side of the brain, and that negative thinking lights up the right side of the brain. It seems that you really can think your way to happiness. We may not be talking rocket science here, but we are talking neuroscience. You can drive yourself crazy, or, you can drive yourself to peace of mind. You can be your own worst enemy or your own best friend. It's your choice. Hey, this one should be a no-brainer.

Michaelangelo, Beethoven, Shakespeare, and Winston

It is important that you invest yourself fully in whatever you choose to do. Do things wholeheartedly. If you do things half-heartedly, your potential satisfaction will be cut in half. If you decide to do something, do it right. Even with work. Maybe, even especially with work. Sam Ewing said, "Hard work spotlights the character of people. Some turn up their sleeves, some turn up their noses, and some don't turn up at all." Taking pride in what you do is related to feeling satisfaction and happiness.

Arthur Winston plans to work as long and as hard as he possibly can. When he started working for the Los Angeles Railway Company at age 17, he was making 41 cents an hour and he and the other blacks had to use separate bathrooms and lunchrooms. He cleaned trolley cars and buses. Blacks weren't allowed to be drivers then. He cleaned the vehicles with vim, vigor, spit, polish, pride, and love. The Los Angeles Railway Company went through many changes and mergers and is now the Metropolitan Transportation Authority (MTA). According to an MTA official, Winston has only missed one day of work. That was the day his wife died. His official work record shows that he never arrived late or left early.

Mr. Winston, by the way, is 98 years old. He's been cleaning buses a long time (you do the math, as the expression goes). Now, he supervises a cleaning crew of nine men and women, and, he's always been warm, friendly, and respectful to his coworkers. Of the MTA's 15 bus and rail yards, only one is named for a person: The Arthur Winston Bus Division.

He believes people shouldn't spend much time thinking about the past. After all, there's work to be done. Yes, Arthur Winston does nothing begrudgingly. His heart is in everything that he does. He believes that worry can kill you, so he lives simply according to his means and focuses on what needs to be done. Mr. Winston is a happy man.

If a man is called to be a street sweeper, he should sweep streets even as Michaelangelo painted, or Beethoven composed music, or Shakespeare wrote poetry. He should sweep streets so well that all the hosts of heaven and earth will pause to say, 'Here lived a great street sweeper who did his job well.'

-Martin Luther King, Jr.

Bruce

My brother Bruce was 11 years older than me. When he was a teenager, there was only one word to describe him: "Cool!" He was in a class by himself. All my other older brothers paled by comparison. He was cooler than James Dean, cooler than Elvis. It seemed that everyone knew his name, and if he didn't know theirs, he'd say, "Hey Chief" or "Hey Champ." My sister, Harriet, was a year or two behind him in the same high school. She said that he was like a celebrity.

From the eyes of a young child (me), he seemed bigger than life. I remember watching him dance around the house before a school dance. His left arm raised out to his side. His right hand in front of his belt buckle. Blue suede shoes. Chartreuse suit. Pegged pants. Gliding around. Cool.

To say that Bruce was a gifted athlete would be an understatement. As a young teen, he'd sometimes score over 40 points in a basketball game when the whole team scored 60 or 65. At age 15, he lied about his age in order to get into the Golden Gloves boxing competition. My brothers Sam and Rip went to see the fight. Bruce's opponent was a huge, muscle-bound guy who appeared to be in his early 20's and had that meaner than a junkyard dog look. The fight was scheduled for three rounds. After a minute of the first round, Bruce was staggered by a series of powerful punches. Blood was flying all over the place. Sam and Rip urged Bruce not to go back out for the second round. They wanted his corner to throw in the towel. Bruce would have none of that. Despite getting battered, he stood toe to toe with that guy for all three rounds. He got his shots in too. Bruce lost the decision.

By age 16, Bruce was a star athlete. In high school, he got varsity letters in football, basketball, baseball, and track. He threw the discus and shot put despite not being a big guy. But he was incredibly strong and his arms felt like steel. In 1950, he was a first team selection for the Reader's Digest All-American Football Team. He never tooted his own horn. He was offered approximately 40 full scholarships but never went to college. But that's a different story for a different time.

Seemingly, the Hollywood type story of Bruce's youth gave way to the complexities of reality. Three wives, five children, and a bunch of grandchildren preceded the lung cancer that was diagnosed in his 69th year. It surprised us all since he never smoked his entire life. We were all there for him, especially Carolee, his loving wife of 20 years, and all of Bruce's kids.

By the time he was diagnosed, the cancer had metastasized and Bruce was terminally ill. He knew it. He asked me directly how much longer he had to live. I told him. He wanted time to square away everything he needed to. When he thought he only had a few months to live, a physician told him he could possibly live another year. He was ecstatic. Can you imagine being told you only had a year left to live, and feeling joy? Well, that's how Bruce reacted. He'd gladly sign up for that year. It was more than he had bargained for. I guess that's an argument for the old saying, "Everything is relative."

Around that time, Bruce told me, "I'm fighting very hard! Giving it all I can!" I had no doubts that was the case. He had discovered what seemed to him to be the secrets of the universe – that there is no such thing as an unimportant day and that life is made up of little moments that we too often take for granted. Like all of us, Bruce wanted more time here, and just like a 15 year old fighting a much more powerful opponent in the Golden Gloves, he gave it his all until there was nothing more to give. He never threw in the towel. When the fight was over and all possible treatments were exhausted, he asked me to help him die. He looked death squarely in the eye and was able to gather and harness the strength, spirit, and wherewithal to ready himself for his passing into what he called "the next world."

He reached that place that so few people ever reach. He went to the abyss. To the precipice. His courage preceded him. He faced everything there was to face. He looked over the edge and stepped off. Bruce died with hope and with integrity. At age 70 he had lived quite a life and had come a long way from those early glory years. But he was still humble and still giving it his all in life and in death. Bruce was still the coolest guy around.

Just Breathin' In, Just Breathin' Out

One of the previous stories emphasized the importance of quieting the mind. One of the best ways of doing so is meditation. Meditation is practice in reducing self-chatter. It is learning how to let go of unnecessary thoughts and how not to be influenced by them. It is not so much of an emptying of the mind as it is a non-judgmental witnessing of what goes on in the mind. It yields a myriad of physiological and psychological benefits.

I have practiced various forms of meditation including Zazen (sitting Zen meditation), transcendental meditation (TM), and clinical standardized meditation. I've also done my homework to hone in on the essential efficacious components of the meditative process. In other words, what actually produces the meditative benefits and what is just fluff and embellishment. The bottom line is that it's easy to do if you follow a few basic instructions:

(1) Find a quiet spot that affords you some privacy. Sit up straight in a chair. Loosen any restrictive clothing. Kick off your shoes if you'd like.

(2) Take note of your breathing. Breathe deeply (not noisily or dramatically). The breath should begin in the area approximately two inches below your belly button. Feel the breath originate. This is the opposite of shallow chest breathing, the type of breathing associated with stress. Take it easy. Each deep breath is taken in through the nose. It is like gently inhaling a narrow stream of air until your belly is full of your inhalation. Then, gently exhale the air through your nose. Long but never strained inhalations and equally lengthy but unstrained exhalations. Just breathin' in, just breathin' out. Just breathin' in, just breathin' out...

(3) With each out breath, silently say the word "one." You are now hooking up a mental device to help you quiet your mind in the early stages of learning how to meditate. It is a mantra equivalent. Each time you exhale, you silently repeat

"one." All your awareness is focused on your breaths and "one."

(4) Inevitably, other thoughts will come into your mind. That's fine. You're not doing anything wrong. As soon as you become aware of anything other than your breathing, you simply let go of it and return your awareness fully to your breathing. It's as if you are a passive, non-judgmental observer of the process you're engaged in. When thoughts arise, you simply return to "one" without any fanfare. The content of your thoughts is totally irrelevant. Every thought is treated exactly the same. It's not good thoughts or bad thoughts. Without judgment, it's just noticing thoughts, letting them go, and returning awareness to breathing. It's always back to "one."

Try this for 10-20 minutes once a day. There's no such thing as a bad meditator as long as you follow the basic instructions outlined above. The benefits are cumulative. As the weeks and months pass, your mind will be less cluttered by the self-babble and typical worries that significantly contribute to unhappiness. The calming down of your mind is like learning how to hang out with yourself without creating problems. It's rather incredible how this very simple process can produce such remarkable benefits. It will change your physiology and your brain waves. Happiness has its own unique biochemistry that contrasts with the biochemistry of unhappiness. Psychologically, you will be breaking old patterns and habits that lead to unhappiness, while establishing new ways of responding that greatly improve your odds of being happy.

Sitting quietly doing nothing,
spring comes and the grass grows by itself.
-Zenrin Kushu

Pavlov's Dog

Sometimes we place unnecessary limits upon ourselves. Maybe we've been conditioned to do so. Everyone who has ever taken a course in general psychology has learned about Pavlov's dog. Pavlov was a psychologist who did experiments in classical conditioning in which he paired the sound of a ringing bell with the feeding of hungry dogs. After awhile, the dogs would salivate to the ringing of the bell alone. They had been conditioned to believe food was coming. Maybe you heard the story about the Avon lady who went to Pavlov's house. The dog ate her.

If we continually pair the same stimulus with the same response, we have conditioned behavior. If a child is always rewarded for staying close to her mommy and daddy, and conversely is subtly or blatantly punished for independent or adventurous behavior, she may grow up feeling insecure and lacking a strong sense of autonomy. She may have difficulty separating from parents and may feel the need to stay close to home. The world may be perceived as a dangerous place and she may feel anxiety if she tries to venture too far from home. She has been conditioned to think, feel, and behave in certain ways.

In India, elephant keepers train baby elephants to stay put by tying a rope, with a stake on the one side, around one leg and placing the stake in the ground. The baby elephant pulls and pulls on the rope to no avail. This teaches the elephant that no matter what he does, he cannot get away when attached to the rope. Later, when the elephant is grown up and the keeper wants the elephant to stay put, all he does is tie a small piece of rope on that leg and the giant elephant is held in place by his own mind.

Such is the phenomenon of conditioning. We learn that X leads to Y and that is that. We behave accordingly, sometimes for a lifetime. I think it's pretty easy to recognize that we can impose limits upon ourselves due to our own conditioned responses. We can and indeed do regularly place limits upon our happiness because of our conditioned belief systems. We've been bombarded from infancy on with messages telling us what we can and can't do, what is appropriate and inappropriate, and what will and won't lead to happiness. We've learned many important lessons but unfortunately we've learned many that prevent us from opening to our potentials.

Being open-minded and being able to change your mind are character strengths that have been identified by Martin Seligman and Christopher Peterson in their work on positive psychology. They realize people can challenge old habits and old styles of negativity by focusing on their character strengths and inculcating new ways of thinking about themselves and the world. What have you been conditioned to believe about yourself, others, and the world that limits you and prevents you from being as happy as possible?

If one places gnats inside a test tube and closes the top, at first the gnats try to jump out and each time they hit the closed top. After about an hour, they give up and one can open the top and the gnats will remain put and eventually die of hunger.

Henny-Penny

Devastating things happen. The axiomatic rug can quickly be pulled out from under us. Our foundation can be shaken to the core. Illness, loss, trauma, terrorism, war, natural disasters, and other worst case scenarios. Threats range from global to our own backyards. We can become disheartened and pessimistic.

If recent history (the last couple of hundred years) has taught us anything, we have learned that we are resilient. We get up off the canvas again and again. Resiliency is positively correlated with life satisfaction. We underestimate how resilient we are. We are survivors. We adapt, evolve, and find a way. That's what we do. That's who we are. That's who you are. Remember that. When you feel like you're coming apart at the seams, you will be able to pull yourself together. You will find a way. You will.

It is important that you understand just how resilient you are. Don't sell yourself short. Challenge any doomsday type thinking. You need time, patience, and determination. In our lifetime and our children's lifetime and their children's lifetime and way beyond that, the world will not come to an end.

It is already tomorrow in Australia.

A boy sat on the wall of the farmyard, idly tossing pebbles.

He threw one and it hit a haystack.

He threw another and it hit the cow who was grazing in a nearby field.

He threw a third and it hit Henny-Penny.

"Dear me!" said Henny-Penny. "The sky is falling. A piece of it hit me on the head. Cluck-cluck, I must go and tell the King!"

So off she went.

"It would be better to sit still and lay an egg," thought the cow to herself. But she said nothing; just went on eating the meadow grass.

"Where are you off to, Henny-Penny?" called Goosey-Poosey from the pond.

"The sky is falling," said Henny-Penny. "A piece of it hit me on the head. Cluck-cluck, I am going to tell the King."

"Whatever will happen next?" said Goosey-Poosey. "I will go with you, Henny-Penny."

So off they went.

"And how will her goslings fare?" thought the cow. But she went on eating the meadow grass.

"Where are you off to, Henny-Penny?" called Cockie-Lockie from his perch on the fence.

"The sky is falling," said Henny-Penny. "We are going to tell the King."

"Good gracious! Is nothing safe? Cock-a-doo, cock-a-doo! I will go with you, Henny-Penny."

So off they went.

"Who now will wake up the day?" thought the cow. But she went on eating the meadow grass.

"Where are you three off to?" asked Foxy-Woxy, slipping out from behind a feather of bracken.

"The sky is falling," said Henny-Penny. "A piece of it hit me on the head. We are going to tell the King."

"A proper and sensible proceeding! He should have the news without delay. I will come with you," said Foxy-Woxy, "and show you a short cut to the palace."

A short cut! How fortunate!

One by one they followed Foxy –Woxy into his dark hole underground. And, snap, snap, snap, went their three heads. They made an excellent breakfast.

"I thought it would come to that," said the cow. But she went on eating the meadow grass.

So Henny-Penny never got to tell the King the sky was falling.

But the King, because he was a king, knew it. He knew the sky is always falling, that dust has closed Helen's eye and that the rain it raineth every day.

And the cow knew it too, and had always known it. But she went on eating the meadow grass.

-As retold by P.L. Travers

The Butterfly Effect

Chaos theory refers to an apparent lack of order in a system that nevertheless obeys particular rules or laws. Its roots stem from the work of Henri Poincare, an early 20th century physicist. There are two primary parts comprising chaos theory. First is that even the most complex systems rely upon underlying order. Secondly, simple or small systems and events can cause very complex behaviors or events. This second idea was presented by Edward Lorenz in a paper presented to the New York Academy of Sciences in 1963. Regarding weather systems, Lorenz proposed that the beating of a butterfly's wings in Brazil might set off a tornado in Texas months later. This quickly became known as "the butterfly effect," and seems to be based on Ray Bradbury's 1952 science fiction story *A Sound of Thunder*, in which a time traveler accidentally steps on a butterfly, changing his entire future.

Here's my question to you: If a butterfly flapping his wings in Brazil can possibly lead to a Texas tornado a few months later, what do you think you really can control? One thing I know for sure is that you can't change what happened five minutes ago and you can't control what happens five minutes from now. My esteemed colleague, Dr. Joseph Luciani, has written extensively on the subject of control. Insecurity leads to a feeling of vulnerability. Wanting to be in control seems constructive but invites problems. As you grow more controlling, you realize that it's an impossible dream to control life. Anxiety, fatigue, depression, and other psychological and physiological maladies permeate your life. Dr. Luciani points out that control is only and always illusion. Here is his antidote: "Develop a reckless attitude of trust." He urges you to stop trying to control life and be courageous enough to live it spontaneously.

Physics tells us there is chaos in the cosmos, in every atom, in the wanderings of every electron. Why should our existence be any different? So, here is our new life philosophy, or at least part of it: Ex-

119

pect, watch for, and embrace uncertainty; dance with the madness of the cosmos, not against it; leave your door open and your heart ready for anything. In this adult world, it may be the only way, not just to survive what is inevitable, but to thrive in the midst of it.

-Vanessa Southern

You may not be able to control life, but it's vital you control what you really can control – your attitude. That's a key ingredient in the happiness solution. Let go of the need to control life. No matter how badly you'd like the world to be a safe and predictable place, it will not unfold according to your expectations or wishes. Embrace the unpredictable by simply accepting it. If something upsetting happens, you'll have plenty of time to worry about it and deal with it. No need to worry in advance. Just trust you'll be able to cope with whatever comes your way, whenever it might occur; your well-being depends on it. Trust in the universe. Trust in yourself.

My life has been filled with terrible misfortunes,
almost all of which never happened.
-Mark Twain

The World According to Freud

Here's the scoop: You can't eat your way to happiness. Most people know that but it doesn't seem to prevent them from trying. Some people are conscious of what they're doing and others are not. Eating out of emotions is common but it doesn't work. If you overeat when you're feeling bored, lonely, or unhappy, it's not a solution to any of those feeling states. I would have no problem with overeating if it provided something resembling a cure. For example, if you were lonely and ate a thousand extra calories, and that solved the issue of loneliness, I'd say, "Bon appetite!" But that's not what happens. What happens is you may get very fleeting pleasurable sensations that take your mind off your loneliness for a brief period of time. Afterwards may come guilt and a sense of having no self-control that you can add to your loneliness. Quite a recipe for unhappiness.

Get more conscious of when you are eating not as a result of physiological hunger but rather as a result of psychologically based feelings. Catch yourself in the act and better yet, learn to catch yourself before the act. It helps to identify the particular feeling rather than to simply know the eating is psychologically based. Is it boredom? How about frustration? Stress? Worry? Anxiety? Anger? Unhappiness? Depression? Guilt? Are you eating because something's "eating away at you?" It's important to identify the feeling that can then lead to your taking specific actions to help resolve the underlying psychological issues connected to your eating when you're not actually hungry for food. It's more likely that you're hungry for activity, attention, company, affection, support, love, or validation.

After identifying the specific feeling, you can begin a plan of correction. Let's say you've identified boredom as the feeling connected to your eating. Recognizing that eating won't solve boredom, you brainstorm on what actually will help to produce less boredom for you. Life isn't boring. You are just making boring choices. Now, instead of doing what you usually do when you feel bored, you come up with a new menu, not of foods, but of actions to take:

(1) Sign up for a community school course.
(2) Join a hiking group.
(3) Read a book from a different genre than you usually do, i.e. biography or history.
(4) Watch a movie from a different genre or era, i.e. science fiction, foreign films, or classic films from the 1940's.
(5) Go work out at the gym.
(6) Call a friend.
(7) Take a walk.
(8) Get a beginning yoga tape/book and try it.
(9) Browse in a bookstore.
(10) Study or research something online that you know little about.
(11) Get involved in a new activity that has a subculture attached to it. For example, if you get involved in running, there are magazines on running and websites as well. There are local running clubs, local road races, and potential running partners in your neighborhood or ones waiting to be found at the road races you attend. It can be similar with many other activities.
(12) Write in a journal. Free associate. Write anything you'd like. Thoughts. Feelings. Poems. Short stories. Your first novel.
(13) Volunteer. Many places would greatly appreciate helping you to be less bored. Volunteers are needed both daytime and nighttime, weekdays or weekends.
(14) Paint, draw, sculpt. Once you've taken an introductory course or two, you're on your way.
(15) Practice the piano or any other musical instrument you'd like to learn.
(16) Plan a day trip and do it. Even working on the plan will help alleviate boredom.
(17) Join the library.
(18) Join a local town or civic organization.
(19) Do activities for your mind such as crossword puzzles, other puzzles, word jumbles, and cryptograms. There

are magazines, books, and websites devoted to these activities.

The ideas I just listed are only the tip of the iceberg. It's virtually impossible to be bored if you do the brainstorming I've suggested. Now, instead of eating when feeling bored, you identify the boredom and go to your menu of things to do rather than your menu of things to eat. If you recognize when you're about to eat because of an emotion, identify the emotion, and institute a plan of correction specifically designed for that emotion, you're going to be a lot happier with yourself.

The three eminent and distinguished psychiatrists, Sigmund Freud, Carl Jung, and Sandor Ferenczi, were on a boat heading from Europe to New York City, where they were to be the keynote speakers at an international conference on psychiatry and mental health. Ferenczi felt seasick and leaned over the side of the boat and threw up. Freud whispered to Jung, "It must be separation anxiety connected to the mother figure, which is now reactivated by his leaving his mother country."

A short time later, it was Jung who became seasick and threw up over the boat's side. Freud whispered to Ferenczi, "It must be repressed aggressive feelings toward his father, stemming from an unresolved Oedipal Complex being reactivated because his conference speech will be competing with mine, and he must see me as a father figure."

Minutes later, it was Freud who felt sick and threw up over the side of the boat. He quickly turned to Jung and Ferenczi and said, "It must have been something I ate."

-Adapted from *Sigmund Freud*, by Ralph Steadman

The Bridge Project

Haworth is a small, neighboring town that I often drive through. As long as I can remember, there's been a narrow, one-lane, wooden plank bridge that goes over the train tracks and connects Haworth to the rest of the world. You can travel across the bridge in either direction, but only one direction at a time. If a car goes west across the bridge, the car going east will have to wait at the bridge's edge for the westbound car to clear before it can make its way across. The whole bridge is about a hundred feet long. It's a bit rickety and every now and again, it is closed for repairs. When it's temporarily shut, people need to take somewhat of a more circuitous or less direct route to their destination. So, I guess it's inconvenient for people when it's not open, and it's inconvenient when it is, because cars always have to wait in one direction for the cars in the other direction. Yet, it's convenient because it offers the most direct route. Somewhat of a mixed bag I guess.

The bridge has been the subject of debate for many decades. Haworth homeowners gather at council meetings to weigh the pros and cons of the bridge. A strong contingent wants to replace the bridge with a newer, improved model that would be wider and allow travel in both directions simultaneously. Ah, a bridge for the 21st century. No wooden planks. Sturdier materials. More efficiency. Finally, the citizens of Smalltown, USA and their municipal administrators agreed on what came to be known as The Bridge Project. Make that seemingly agreed.

It wasn't long before yellow signs with bold, black letters began appearing on people's lawns. A few here. A few there. The signs simply said, "Rethink The Bridge Project." With each passing week, the number of signs increased, as more and more Haworth residents agreed to signs being placed on their front yards. It was literally a grassroots movement. It became apparent that rethinking the bridge project was something worth considering.

Don't throw away the old bucket until
you know whether the new one holds water.
-Swedish Proverb

I have to admit that I like the bridge just the way it is, with all its flaws and blemishes. I don't mind waiting my turn to cross it. I like its uniqueness and that it's the only one lane bridge I've come across in this area. It's functional. It's a work of art. I'm used to it. It's always been there, steady and reliable, kind of like a good friend. Sort of reminds me of my buddy, Sal. We've been friends about 50 years. There's history there. Walked to school together. Got kicked out of the neighborhood club together. Started our own club. Played stickball, basketball, street football, and hung on the corner together.

Right before our high school graduation, I took Sal's yearbook and kept it overnight so I'd have the time to write something lengthy, thoughtful, and reflective of our friendship. He took my yearbook also. I wrote a full page of sentimental remembrances and wishes. The next day, we returned the yearbooks to each other. What Sal wrote in my book stunned me. It was, "Best Wishes, Sal." I have to admit that it was and still is quite funny. Forty-three years later, Sal and I went through the entire yearbook page by page as we tried to decide whether to attend our high school reunion. Sal and I once played a game of 500 rummy to about a hundred thousand points. Tried and true, like the Haworth bridge.

I recently came across an old cardboard shoebox from 1969. I had put some items of interest in the box and put it away, only to be rediscovered 36 years later. There were letters in there from important people in my life who had taken the time to try to cheer me up. I was in the army at the time. One of the letters was from Sal. Seeing his handwriting reminded me of the notes we'd pass back and forth while sitting next to each other in the high school auditorium during "study hall."

My wife Nan and I have dinner once a month or so with Sal and his wife, Toni, and it's always a good time. In difficult times, they are there for us, and we for them. It takes about an hour to get from our house to theirs, and we have to cross the Haworth bridge to get there. Friendships bridge different phases of our lives. To have a good friend, you need to be a good friend. Friendships that work and have stood the test of time will help you to feel happier.

If your friendships are fine, consider yourself fortunate. If they are not, try to bridge the gap. If I lived in Haworth, there would be a sign on my lawn, and it would boldly proclaim:

Rethink The Bridge Project

On Hawaii, Alaska, and the 47 Contiguous States – Reprisal

One of the stories appearing in my previous book was entitled "On Hawaii, Alaska, and the 47 Contiguous States." It had to do with a game my wife, children, and myself played while driving on long car trips. We tried to find license plates for all fifty states. When the game started, Dave and Jen were ten years old. Let me recap a bit of the original story:

Not once in eleven years has a North Dakota license plate appeared. Last year, we even briefly considered vacationing to North Dakota so as to finally reach a resolution to our eleven-year itch. Saner heads prevailed as we quickly ruled out that possibility. We thought about writing or calling people in North Dakota and having them send old plates or at least a picture of their license plates. We decided to wait it out and play fair and square.

I'm a patient person and recognize that things sometimes happen for a reason. Keeping in mind the old Ecclesiastes line that "there's a time for everything under the sun", I figured that we didn't need to do anything dramatic and when the time is right we could discover that elusive license plate.

Yesterday, I was sitting at a traffic light in our home town and suddenly got a very intense, almost bordering on the mystical, sensation that the van pulling next to me at the light was from North Dakota. I would let it pull away first when the light changed green so that I could get a good look at it. Finally, it pulled out and I got a look at the plate. And there it was...a New Jersey plate. Not exactly the kind of miracle I'd been looking for, but it did put a smile on my face as I thought of the Zen teaching of finding the miraculous in the ordinary.

The ordinary, the pedestrian, the typical day to day sights and sounds that we take for granted. A New Jersey plate right here in New Jersey. Of course! Will miracles never cease?

I'm happy to report that the game officially came to an end when my wife Nan and I spotted a car with North Dakota plates driving through our neighborhood. We were screaming like little kids. We were entitled. After all, we had waited a long time. During our wait:

- George Bush, Sr. was President.
- Cell phones, laptop computers, and surfing the web embraced children, adults, and seniors.
- Lance Armstrong won seven Tour De France races.
- Clinton served two terms.
- Seinfeld had its entire run of nine years.
- Several wars were fought.
- The younger Bush took office.
- Y2K and the millennium came and went.
- 9/11 shocked us.
- Homeland Security began.
- Hurricane Katrina devastated New Orleans.

The list could go on and on. Dave and Jen were 23 years old when the game finished, and if truth be told, they had very little interest in it the last ten years or so. Nan and I kept it going, taking it as a challenge of sorts. (Are you saying, "Get a life!" as you read this?)

Fast forward to the summer of 2005. The four of us are traveling to a wedding outside of Boston when Nan decides she's going to do a reprisal of the old license plate game. We quickly see Connecticut, New York, Rhode Island, Massachusetts, and Indiana. To our surprise, Iowa and Louisiana are spotted. And then, there it is – North Dakota. What took us over 13 years the first time around was now accomplished within hours. More support for the "you never know" philosophy of life.

When I studied with the noted Zen Master, Soen Sa Nihm, he would always remind me to keep "don't know mind." The first few times he said it with his rather thick accent, I thought he was saying "donut mind," and tried to understand the symbolic meaning that must be attached to that phrase. Then, I realized it was actually "don't know mind." I think this was his way of letting me know that I shouldn't be surprised at anything that happens, and that I should have no expectations. The world will never unfold exactly as you think. Have goals and values and high standards. Have dreams. Persevere. But let go of your expectations. Just do your best and let go. To the degree that there is a gap between your expectations and your experiences, you will increase your levels of frustration, disappointment, and discontentedness. North Dakota took over 13 years. North Dakota took less than a day. You'll be happier if you keep "don't know mind," or "donut mind," whichever you'd prefer.

Impersonating a Doctor

Years ago, I drove an old Toyota...and drove it and drove it and drove it. Reliable transportation, but not much to look at. It could have been appropriately referred to as a "rustmobile." On those occasions when my daughter, Jenna, missed the bus, I'd drive her to school. When we got there, she'd kind of slither down in the passenger seat to reduce the chances of anyone seeing her. Inevitably, I'd beep the horn and wave to her friends and teachers. Humility is a valuable lesson to learn. It's interesting that the words humility and humiliation have the same root. I'm going to have to look that up.

One crisp, fall afternoon when I had no scheduled appointments, I decided to go to my office at the Riverside Medical Building and catch up on paperwork. I've never had a secretary and have always been responsible for all aspects of my private practice, including billing, typing, and so on. Dressed in naturally faded blue jeans and a worn flannel shirt, I pulled my trusty Toyota into the parking lot. I grabbed my typewriter (no computer in the office at the time) and walked toward the entrance at the back of the building. The door to get in was stuck in a position that kept it open three or four inches. It wouldn't budge, so I couldn't close it. The four urologists on the top floor own the building and I assumed they would take care of it.

After laboring through seven hours of catching up and typing (or something resembling that skill) numerous reports, it was time to go home. It was about 9:30 p.m. and I was most likely the only person left in the building. I grabbed the typewriter, closed my office, and began to leave the building. As I got to the door leading to the parking lot, I noticed that the door was still stuck in an open position. No one had fixed it. My car was the only one in the entire parking lot and I started walking toward it. Suddenly, a police car screeched into the lot. Evidently, the officer had seen me through the glass doors in the front of the building as he was driving by. He pulled next to me and asked, "What are you doing here?"

I responded, "My office is in this building. I was just leaving." He eyed me up and down. There I was dressed very casually (perhaps shabbily) and was leaving a medical building late at night carrying a typewriter.

He asked with more than a moderate degree of skepticism, "You're a doctor?"

I said, "Yes, I've been in this building a long time. I have my business card in my wallet if you'd like to see it."

He nodded affirmatively. I took out my wallet and searched to no avail. Not one card was to be found. He looked at me suspiciously and asked, "What happened to the door?" Yes, a broken door and me carrying a typewriter late at night. Then the officer eyed the "rustmobile." "And that's your car?"

"Yes, that's mine," I answered.

"And, you're a doctor?" he said in such a way that what he was probably thinking was that this guy needs a doctor.

"I am. I'm a psychologist here. I have a key for the door (pointing to the door that was stuck in an open position). He asked me to show him the key. He took it and put it in the lock. Needless to say, it didn't work. I guess the entire door, including the lock, was malfunctioning. At this point, he called for back-up. Not only did I not look like a doctor, or drive a car that a doctor would drive, there was a broken door, an ill-fitting key, the typewriter, the missing business card... I couldn't blame him for calling other officers to join him.

More recently, on a late March morning, in the middle of a blizzard, I set out to drive my daughter to Newark airport to catch a flight that would take her to her spring break destination. The roads were treacherous, but we managed to get there. I dropped Jenna at the terminal and went to park the car. It was a long walk back in the heavy snow and high winds. My beard, which was longer than it had been in many years, was rearranged by the elements and icicles formed in it. When I got inside the terminal, my daughter, in tears, informed me that all the flights were cancelled. She called her boyfriend whom she was supposed to meet at her spring break destination. He got on the computer and claimed there was a flight leaving LaGuardia later that afternoon that had not been cancelled. If possible, the weather conditions were worsening, but we decided to try to get to LaGuardia.

The wipers were frozen, and in trying to fix them, I broke them. At times I had to drive with my head halfway out the window, but we made it. Again, I dropped her off, parked the car, and made the trek to the terminal. By the time I made it there, I'm not sure what I looked like, but I'm certain it wasn't a pretty sight. I found my daughter (in tears again) and she told me the flight was delayed and would probably be cancelled. They were not going to sell any tickets until a disposition was made at approximately 6:00 p.m. We waited. They finally sold tickets and Jenna had to go to the boarding area. That was when we separated, roughly 6:15. Not owning a cell phone at the time, our communication was cut off at that point. I was not going to leave the airport, being it was still possible her flight would be cancelled. Just about every flight had been cancelled, so the airport was now relatively empty. Still delayed. It was 7:30, then 8:20, and 9:30. I kept asking airport personnel about the flight. Nobody had definitive information. I continued to ask. There were eight or nine airline workers gathered at the area where I earlier had to leave my daughter. I asked about her flight. I knew the flight number and destination and continued to try to find out if it would take off or be cancelled.

I walked the length of the terminal as I waited. I walked it more than once. I sat in a chair and started to meditate. In a flash, I was surrounded by four armed police officers. One of them requested that I remain seated and instructed me not to make any sudden moves. He said there had been several reports of a suspicious looking man asking a lot of questions about a flight and that I matched the description of that man. The fact of my being tall, thin, dark and bearded didn't help. I was perceived as an Osama Bin Laden looking character. They asked me many questions, checked my ID, and took steps to verify that my daughter was actually a passenger on the flight I'd been so interested in.

The irony of the situation struck me. Four fairly young black males (police officers) were doing to me what they've probably had done to themselves on various occasions. It was a type of racial or ethnic profiling. Young black males are sometimes the recipients of prejudice, pigeonholing, and the like. Now, it was my turn. I was a book being judged by its cover. The common denominator with respect to the suspicious police at Riverside Medical and the police in the airport was that I did not appear to fit their notions of what I was supposed to look like or how I was supposed to behave, although I had not behaved badly at all in either situation.

Research on happiness has found that people who display traits of open-mindedness and fairness are happier than those who are more closed-minded, smug, or prejudiced. A good exercise is to try and relate differently to people whom you typically would not relate much to at all. If you meet a person that doesn't attract you physically or stimulate you intellectually, don't dismiss them or be sold on the idea that they have nothing to offer you. Keep an open mind. A first impression isn't always the best indicator of what a person is like or if that person and you can share time and space in a mutually satisfying way. I was neither the burglar nor the terrorist. I was simply working hard in the one situation, and a concerned father in the other. Give people a chance by giving yourself a chance to get to know them, despite their appearance or your initial judgment of them. Recognize how your own fears, biases, and conditioning all limit your potential to be more engaged with others in satisfying ways. Make an effort not to stereotype or pigeonhole others. Look beyond appearances.

My daughter's flight took off at 10:40, about 13 hours after we started out that morning. It was almost midnight by the time I got home. It turned out to be quite a day. Not exactly what we thought it would be like. I thought about a passage I like that was written by Ralph Waldo Emerson:

> I am thankful for small mercies. I compared notes with one of my friends who expects everything of the universe, and is disappointed when anything is less than the best, and I found that I begin at the other extreme, expecting nothing, and am always full of thanks for moderate goods.

Seeing Is Believing?

I woke out of a dream this morning asking myself the question, "If you were standing on your head, would the world just look upside down or would it actually be upside down?" No, I'm not making this up. It really happened. You know what they say about truth being stranger than fiction. Anyhow, before you ask, "Why are you pondering such an inane question?" and, "Don't you have anything better to do with your time?" let me expound a bit on the subject.

To reiterate, if you were standing on your head, would the world look upside down, or, would it actually be upside down? This is not a question of semantics. It's phenomenology, physics, philosophy, and, more to the point, it's psychology. You see, this is what happens to us day in and day out. We put ourselves in certain positions that determine how we perceive our world. And, we believe our perceptions are gospel, rather than realizing our perceptions are related to the positions we put ourselves in.

Jennifer put herself in the position of trying to please everyone. She was accommodating, pliable, and would go out of her way routinely to do things for people. She relegated her own needs and wishes, in essence, neglecting herself while making sure she took care of everyone else. Jennifer put herself in the position of doormat. After years of being in that position, her experience of the world was the following: It was a cruel world in which she felt taken advantage of. She felt used and that everyone was better than her (above her) and that no one paid enough attention to her or gave her any respect. It's not easy being a doormat.

Jennifer needed to learn that she was not a doormat, but a worthwhile and lovable human being who assumed the position of doormat because she was trying to get certain basic needs satisfied. But, assuming that position gave her a distorted view of the world and led to a "poor me, everyone is walking all over me" feeling about herself and life. Was the world really like that or was it just that Jennifer's world was like that because of the position she put herself into? So, if you were standing on your head, would the world be upside down or would it just look and feel upside down?

Another position of interest is when someone is "sitting on top of the world." I could just as easily have woken out of the dream this morning asking myself the question, "If you're sitting on top of the world, is the world really beneath you or does it just seem and feel that way?" I would guess that if you're on top of the world, your view could be a bit skewed. Are people beneath you? Do you need their adulation? I'm always a bit amused when athletes and celebrities refer to themselves in the 3rd person. No, I can't imagine that the view is entirely clear when you're sitting on top of the world.

What about the position of sitting in the director's chair? You know best. You know how people should think, feel, and behave. Your way is the right way. Others' methods pale by comparison. There's only one way to skin a cat. There's your way or the wrong way. You're constantly surprised when people say or do the things they do. You're routinely disappointed with others. You shake your head and wonder. "What is it with them and why don't they get it?" The world (outside of you) seems inept and like they're proceeding by the seat of their pants. People think you're controlling, but they don't really understand – you really do know best! So, if you're sitting in the director's chair, is the world really running amok without you taking charge and directing the show, or does it just appear that way to you?

We put ourselves in positions that we become entrenched in. From those positions, we perceive the world in certain ways and thus act accordingly. The world we create for ourselves is in a large part related to the position we decide to assume in order to view it.

If you are less than happy, consider the possibility of changing the position that you put yourself in on a daily basis simply because that's the position you know best. Do whatever it takes to put yourself in a different position. For example, try asserting yourself appropriately, or practice humility, or relinquish control. In other words, challenge the status quo and try a position that works better for you rather than the same one that leads to perceptual distortion and unhappiness.

I was giving a patient the Rorschach Inkblot Test. Each inkblot may resemble something specific such as a butterfly or two dancing bears, or more likely the blots do not look like anything in particular. There really are no right or wrong answers. It's considered a projective test in which the responses are thought to be psychologically revealing. When I showed him the first card he responded with, "I see a naked woman." On the second inkblot he replied similarly. "It's a naked woman." On card three, he said, "More of the same Doc – two naked women."

Prior to showing him the remaining inkblots, I said to him, "I notice that you seem to have a specific interest in naked women. Can you tell me more about that?"

My patient spontaneously answered, "Don't ask me, Doc. You're the one who's showing all the dirty pictures!"

Oh, What Tangled Webs We Weave

Dishonesty is an impediment to happiness. Lying interferes with relationships and lowers self-esteem. Jobs are lost and marriages break up as a result of deceit. Lies create tension and breed mistrust. I'm not encouraging brutal honesty. You are entitled to private thoughts and feelings. It does damage to impulsively express all of your feelings and thoughts in the name of honesty.

You know the difference between brutal honesty (used as a weapon) and honesty (sincere, truthful communication not used as ammunition, but rather as an attempt to inform, clarify, or educate in hopes of dealing effectively with a person and/or situation). It may appear as if lying is helpful or aiding you in getting what you want, but it's usually just a matter of time until the proverbial feces hits the proverbial fan.

The Mullah was giving a party for his friends and bought six pounds of the finest lamb to be served for dinner. His wife was a wonderful cook and he asked her to prepare it as only she could. After cooking the lamb, she tasted it and it was without a doubt the tastiest meal that she had ever prepared. She ate it all by herself. That night when the Mullah arrived home, his wife told him that he needed to buy more meat because the cat had eaten it all. The Mullah became suspicious and got his scale. He weighed the cat. It weighed exactly six pounds. He asked his wife, "If this is the cat, where is the meat? And if this is the meat, where is the cat?"
-Sufi Wisdom

Of course, the best way of learning to be honest is to work on living your life in a way in which you're not creating guilt, shame, or embarrassment. The goal is to feel happy. Decisions and actions that leave you struggling with feeling ashamed, embarrassed, or guilty are taking you in the wrong direction. Before getting yourself involved in circumstances that you feel it will be necessary to be dishonest about, think carefully again and again. Impulsive actions that may temporarily give you pleasure will most likely not bring you happiness. There is a difference between pleasure and happiness.

On the first of each month, the Mullah would cross the border with thirty donkeys, each of which carried two bales of straw. Each time, the customs agent would ask the Mullah's profession, and the Mullah would reply, "I am an honest smuggler." So each time, the Mullah and his donkeys and the bales of straw would be searched from top to bottom. Each time, the customs agent would not find anything. This went on every month for many years. And so it was that every time the Mullah, his donkeys, and the bales of straw were searched, nothing could be found.

Many years later, both the Mullah and the custom agent retired. One day, the two adversaries happened to meet in a country far from home. They hugged each other like old buddies. After chatting for awhile, the customs agent asked the question that had haunted him for decades.

"Mullah, please tell me what you were smuggling all those years!"

The Mullah thought for a few seconds, and finally gave the long awaited answer. "Donkeys."

Dulcinea

Prior to the first day of elementary school, a teacher was told that five of her students were gifted and were leaders. What she wasn't told was that this was a research study, and that the psychologists had chosen the five kids randomly. In reality, the designated children had no more intelligence or talent than the other kids. The teacher, however, believed them to be special. At the end of the school year, the teacher did evaluations of all her pupils. The five that were supposedly gifted scored higher on most variables than the others. I don't think this is the placebo effect or the old self-fulfilling prophecy. After all, the kids didn't even know they were labeled in such positive terms. I'd call it more of a Dulcinea effect. Let me explain.

Alonso Quejana was a retired, middle-aged gentleman living in the Spanish village of la Mancha. He was an avid reader and was obsessed with chivalrous ideas. He was a true romantic. In Cervante's book, we follow the transformation of Alonso as he evolves into Don Quixote de la Mancha, the errant knight who fights windmills and defends his ideals. It's hard to write about this without singing, "I'm Don Quixote, the man of la Mancha..." Go ahead, sing it, it's okay. This is a book about feeling good. Belt it out. Sing it as if no one is listening. Like you would in the shower. Anyway, back to the story.

Aldonza Lorenzo is a peasant girl, but Don Quixote believes she is a princess. He believes it not simply intellectually, but with his heart and soul, and with every fiber of his being. He believes she is the princess Dulcinea (sweetness). Much of the plot of Don Quixote is about his travels with Sancho Panza, a rustic farmer who became Don's faithful squire. Sancho understands that Dulcinea may not really exist, and that Aldonza is simply a peasant. But Don Quixote will have none of that. He is more interested in dreaming the impossible dream and righting the unrightable wrong. He is a romantic in love, a man with a mission, and a believer in Dulcinea.

In essence, Aldonza Lorenzo, the peasant girl, became the princess Dulcinea because Don Quixote believed in her to the degree that he did. I think the elementary school teacher believed in the five kids and they became what they were capable of becoming. The Dulcinea effect.

Believe in someone. Tarzan had Jane. Ozzie had Harriet. Charlie Brown had the little red haired girl. The story of Don Quixote de la Mancha and his princess Dulcinea is also about being courageous enough to have dreams and pursue them. Whatever Dulcinea represents, she is life enhancing and worth pursuing. I hope there's a Dulcinea in your life, be it a person, a dream, a cause, or anything that you believe is worth believing in. I think you'll be happier if you believe that strongly in someone or something.

At the end of the story, Don Quixote was ill and on his deathbed. He no longer believed he was a knight or that there ever was a Dulcinea. In an effort to inspire him, Sancho reminded him of Dulcinea, but he replied, "I was mad and now I am sane. I was Don Quixote de la Mancha, and now I am, as I have said, Alonso Quejana..." He dictated his will and died. Believe in someone. Believe in yourself. Dream big, and keep the fire burning. Sing it again. Sing it with me. "I'm Don Quixote, the man of la Mancha..."

Mind Over Matter

Krige Schabort was the men's winner in the 2003 New York City Marathon. Wheelchair division. Both of his legs were blown off during the war in Angola. During a television interview, he said, "Most of all, I'm happy to be alive. I can be that far from dead (holding thumb and index finger very close together), but I won't give up. My mental ability is my most powerful weapon." By mental ability, Schabort was not referring to his intelligence level. He meant the ability to use his mind to help him become the best he could be at marathoning and in life in general. He stated, "My ultimate goal is to be the best father and best husband I can be." Based on his own account and the accounts of those who know him well, Krige Schabort is happy.

Marla Runyan is another excellent runner and marathoner. She runs with grace, power, and confidence. She has been legally blind since age nine. Runyan has Stargardt's disease. It's an incurable form of macular degeneration that eclipses central vision. Some peripheral vision is maintained and she uses that, along with instinct, crowd noise, and various other subtle multi-sensory cues to keep her on course. Runyan has been quoted as saying, "I think what I represent is achieving what you want in life. It's a matter of your attitude. Some people have a negative attitude, and that's their disability."

Please read that last line again. Once more. It's an important line, especially when we are talking about happiness or the lack of it. Runyan agrees with Schabort about how vital it is to harness your mind's power to work for you rather than against you. Marla Runyan would most likely prefer good vision to blindness. Krige Schabort would most likely prefer to have his legs back. Their stories could have been different than they are. But, both Marla and Krige are happy. Bertrand Russell once said, "To be without some of the things you want is an indispensable part of happiness." My hunch is that owners of Rolls Royces and Porsches are no happier than owners of Fords. It's pretty much guaranteed that you'll never have everything that you want, and I think that's the way it needs to be if you're to develop appreciation, compassion, hope, humility, gratitude, and other character traits that are routinely found in happy people. Get that mind working for you, not against you. You may not be blind or without legs, but you can take some clues from Krige and Marla.

> When one door of happiness closes, another opens;
> but often we look so long at the closed door that we
> don't see the one that has opened for us.
> -Helen Keller

At the Zoo

When I was immortal and was a junior in college, 36 of my closest friends and I rented a house at the Jersey shore. The plan was to party hardy for the summer. We aptly named the house (and its collection of characters) "The Zoo." On the first official Saturday of the summer, adorned in t-shirts imprinted with "The Zoo," all 37 of us arrogantly marched to the beach accompanied by several bagpipers. We were what's happening, as the saying goes. We were full of bluster and full of ourselves. We danced on the beach, played our music as loud as we wanted, and had something resembling a total disregard for our neighbors. It took about a week for the shore town of Bradley Beach to have the Board of Health condemn our house and get us out of town. The Zoo was closed. That was over 40 years ago. I guess there is a time and place for everything. Or, is there?

Each year, people in their 70's and 80's decide to get their high school equivalency degrees and/or start college. Ninety year olds complete the New York Marathon. Five year olds work diligently to raise money for charities. Centenarians do volunteer work at medical centers. My 12 year old niece just got braces and a new bike. When I turned 60, I got braces and a new bike. So, maybe there isn't a specific time and place for everything.

About ten years ago, a good friend of mine, who lives in San Francisco, was down and out. His business had failed and he lost all his savings in the market. He was depressed and wasn't eating well or sleeping much. One evening, trying to pull himself together and make a new start, he shaved and put on a classy business suit. He went to a very expensive five star restaurant and was treated royally as he ate course after course. He sipped the finest wine, sampled the caviar, had pheasant under glass, and crème de boulet. When he finished his after-dinner coffee with brandy, the waiter presented him with the check. My friend had no money and informed the waiter of his plight. The waiter called over the maitre'd. They called over other restaurant personnel. They grabbed my seemingly unremorseful friend by the back of the collar of his suit and tossed him out of the restaurant, just like you would see on television.

It took about a decade, but my resourceful friend decided to return to the scene of the crime, so to speak. Feeling good about himself, he went back to that same restaurant. Once again, he ate like a king, not passing up a course. He ordered a bottle of the best French champagne. Escargot. Duck l'orange. Chocolate mousse. Café au lait and apricot brandy. As it turned out, the same maitre'd still worked there. My friend called him over and said, "You don't remember me, do you?"

The maitre'd replied, "No, monsieur, I do not."

My friend told him the story of what happened ten years earlier and how the maitre'd had him thrown out of the restaurant. The maitre'd was extremely embarrassed and apologized profusely.

"I am so sorry, monsieur. Please forgive me. Thank you for coming back again. I am very sorry. Please forgive me."

My friend nodded and said, "It's okay, I just wanted to let you know I'm ready to be thrown out again."

The idea that there's a time and a place for everything seems very rigid and limiting for me. Taking things out of their typical categories and time frames expands possibilities and the potential for increasing zest, a flexible mind, and humor, all of which are associated with being happy. For example, there are not breakfast foods (only to be eaten in the morning), lunch foods, and dinner foods. There is food. You can eat vegetables for breakfast or cereal at dinnertime. School doesn't have to stop when you're in your 20's and work doesn't have to stop when you're 65. I like to think that you can teach an old dog new tricks, and that a puppy or an old dog can teach you a thing or two as well. So, is there a time and a place for everything? I think that there probably is, and I'm certain that there really isn't. Improvise, play, be responsible and respectful, enjoy the scenery and accept the paradoxical. Don't take yourself too seriously and keep yourself open to the joy of every phase of life.

Smile

On a beautiful spring morning, myself and two of my siblings went to the cemetery where my brother Sam is buried. It was Sam's birthday, his first since his death. After a considerable amount of time that allowed for each of us to privately express ourselves, I stood in front of the grave and motioned for my brother and sister to join me. I draped an arm over each of their shoulders and asked, "Are you ready?" They looked puzzled. I began to sing very softly, "Happy birthday to you, happy birthday to you, happy birthday dear Sammy, happy birthday to you."

Having no real expectations in that situation, I was not terribly disappointed when they both immediately informed me how appalled they were by my singing (not my voice, but by the fact that I was singing happy birthday to my deceased brother). They actually shook their heads from side to side as if to say, "How could you?" or, "What's wrong with you?" I explained to them that I was just doing what we all did when Sam was alive. We would meet for lunch, light a small candle shaped like a cake, and would all softly sing happy birthday to Sam. And, Sam would join in as well, and it was a tradition of sorts. I didn't see why we couldn't continue to sing to Sam, and I envisioned his joining in and enjoying the whole thing. Despite my explanation, my sister and brother didn't seem to get it. Maybe they thought it was disrespectful or that cemeteries just weren't arenas for song. It didn't turn into an argument. It's fine that they felt differently about it than I did.

Around that same time frame, I began working with a young woman who was suffering with anxiety attacks. They interfered with her ability to do her job effectively. She felt frightened and discouraged. Her "poppy" (grandfather) had recently died. She had been very close to him. She was worried about her parents and said, "My family is unraveling." Lisa felt as if the loss was too much to bear. I knew her pain and her fears. We spoke about life from a philosophical perspective. We worked on developing tools and the wherewithal to reduce and deal with her anxiety. She was smart, creative, and had deep faith. She began to realize that it was less that her family was unraveling and was more that everything changes, including her family. Things are always in flux. Is it unraveling or evolving?

I urged her to continue her relationship with her poppy. He was still available to her. She could visit him at the cemetery, talk to him, seek his advice, or write to him. I let her know that my dad died thirty some odd years ago and that I still have an ongoing relationship with him, and still talk to him. She understood that this was not about denial or pathological mechanisms. She and I had both grieved our losses. This was about not getting stuck in the spot of being unable to move on. She had had a great relationship with her poppy. We spoke of the need to accept the inescapable fact of his death and also accept the inescapable fact of the life and time she had with him. With regard to her poppy, I told her to smile because it happened. Because it happened in the first place. It, being her relationship with him. Smile because it happened.

That's how I feel when I think of Sam. How blessed I was to have him as my brother. When I think of Sam, I feel happy, just as Lisa does when she thinks of her poppy. By the way, the following spring, my brother and sister and I once again went to the cemetery on Sam's birthday. I smiled when my sister suggested that we sing happy birthday to Sam.

The Search

A recent Gallup poll found that 85% of Americans believe spirituality is important. Just about every culture has some belief in a force, an ultimate power, or the transcendent. Searching for what is sacred adds purpose and meaning to many people's lives. However, most people get side-tracked and use their energies in search of other things that they equate with happiness and the good life. Roger Walsh, in his book *Essential Spirituality*, discusses the search for happiness in our culture:

> What leads to true happiness? A glance at our possessions and priorities, our society and media, makes it very apparent what most people believe will bring true happiness: things – and lots of them. Each billboard and neon sign, every radio and television wails forth a siren song suggesting that if we just buy this, own that, taste this, then real contentment will finally be ours. Our culture is fixated on the physical foursome of money, sensuality, power, and prestige – we are lost in the seductive illusion that if we can somehow just get enough of them, we will finally be fully and forever happy.

Studies have been done to determine which countries have the highest percentage of happy people. A team of researchers from the London School of Economics found that, despite its enormous wealth, the United States ranked only 46th in the list of so-called happiest countries. Let me surprise you by mentioning some of the countries that finished with a higher percentage of happy inhabitants. Croatia, Estonia, Ghana, and Latvia. Really. Did you raise your eyebrows? It turns out that two of the world's happiest countries are Bangladesh and India, countries where the curbing of material desires is taught.

It may be that the United States emphasizes pleasure as promoting happiness. Pleasurable sensations and experiences may be part of the picture, but there's got to be a lot more to it than that. In his book *Authentic Happiness*, Martin Seligman discusses three components of happiness – pleasure, engagement, and meaning. "Engagement" refers to a passionate depth of involvement with family, friends, work, and interests. "Meaning" has to do with harnessing your personal strengths to serve some larger end. It turns out that engagement and meaning are much more important than pleasure with respect to what it takes to live a happy and fulfilled life.

Are there shortcuts to happiness? Not really. Taking drugs, making loads of money, engaging in mindless entertainment, using the most popular cologne, wearing designer clothes, playing video games and the like may all increase your pleasure but are only third tier players in producing happiness. I like Seligman's term describing what it's like to simply focus on pleasure rather than engagement and meaning. He calls it the "fidgeting until death" syndrome.

Heed the words of Greg Easterbrook, writing in a special issue of *Time* magazine that dealt with the science of happiness:

> ...the things that really matter in life are not sold in stores. Love, friendship, family, respect, a place in the community, the belief that your life has purpose – those are the essentials of human fulfillment, and they cannot be purchased with cash. Everyone needs a certain amount of money, but chasing money rather than meaning is a formula for discontent.

There's nothing wrong with having a lot of money. Money can make life easier, but it's not a very large part of the happiness solution. Not only can you not buy happiness, you can't even rent it or lease it. It's not about possessions. I don't think anyone really resolved a mid-life crisis by buying a sports car (although millions have tried). Get off the making more and more money treadmill. Give up the quest to obtain what the sly Madison Avenue advertising companies tell you that you need in order to be worthy and desirable. It's all illusion and has little to do with happiness. It's not about Gucci. It's not about the Hummer. It's about believing in a cause, having a purpose, getting connected. It's about charity, religion or spirituality (atheists included), and altruism. It's about love, family, friends, and depth of engagement. It's about quieting your mind, becoming less cynical and less bitter. It's about reaching in and reaching out. Less resentment, more forgiveness. Less blame, more compassion. Less fear, more acceptance. It's about giving up your illusions and really seeing what contributes to happiness. It's accessing your spiritual self. It's searching for the sacred.

I'm Not Religious, But...

I am not religious. At least I wouldn't describe myself as being religious in the typical sense of the word. I was raised in a Jewish family, but we never went to the synagogue except for rare occasions. I didn't go to Hebrew school, but had a few private sessions with a rabbi and learned enough to get bar mitzvahed. My wife, Nan, is Syrian Orthodox. We got married in the 1960's around the time of an Arab-Israeli war. I had a fleeting thought that I might be assassinated at my wedding. It was a civil ceremony and all went smoothly.

Actually, we attempted to get both a priest and a rabbi to officiate at the wedding, but neither was interested. In fact, they left us with a sense that they believed we were doing something wrong, and that our chances of having a lasting and happy marriage were infinitesimal. To be honest, our families were skeptical and less than thrilled, particularly Nan's parents. Nan insists it had less to do with religion and more to do with the fact that I was a private in the army making $87 per month (but that's a separate story you'll read later in this book). My opinion is that it had more to do with religion. One of my older brothers, Sam, warned me against the marriage, telling me it would only be a matter of time before she called me a dirty Jew. It never happened. Sam, Nan and I joked about it many years later.

My personal experiences were suggesting to me that religion could be the great divider of peoples. It seemed paradoxical. I would think religion could be the great common denominator of people, but it just didn't seem to work that way. All throughout my childhood and adolescence, we moved frequently and were always one of the lone Jewish families in our neighborhood. My formative years were scarred by blatant anti-Semitism and I was frequently called a "Jew bastard" or "kike."

In the 1970's, I became fascinated with Zen Buddhism. It struck me as the antithesis of divisive religion. I was drawn to its non-dogmaticism. I took classes, visited Zen temples, meditated regularly, and had encounters with Zen Masters. To me, Zen was inclusive, not exclusive. The Korean Zen Master, Soen Sa Nimh, told the following story that I resonated with immediately upon hearing it:

> In a cookie factory, cookies come in all different forms. Some are large and others small. They may be shaped like stars, people, animals, or buses, but they are all made from the same dough. It's all the same substance although the cookies appear quite different. And so it is with you and me and people who appear so different. We're all made from the same dough.

In the late 1970's, I had a conversation with a friend who had become a born again Christian. We spent an hour talking about religion. I remember the exchange vividly. He stated emphatically that the only way a person can get to heaven is by accepting Jesus Christ as his Savior. I presented the following scenario to John: "What if someone was an absolutely wonderful human being who was essentially selfless and devoted her life to helping others? Suppose this person did lots of charitable work, lived by the golden rule, and was loving in all possible ways. And, let's suppose she happened to be a Hindu or Jew or Buddhist or Muslim or of any religion that believed Jesus was a great prophet, but not the one and only son of God. And then, let's say there was a man who was cruel hearted, selfish, and created a wake of destruction wherever he went. He molested children and ripped off senior citizens, but had an epiphany shortly before he died and accepted Jesus Christ as his savior. Who goes to heaven?"

John didn't miss a beat. He quickly and confidently answered, "The man who accepted Jesus as his savior goes to heaven. The woman doesn't." Where do you go from there? I'm thankful to report that a recent study found that 79% of poll respondents believe that someone of another faith can "attain salvation or go to heaven." Phew!

If you wonder where I'm going with all this, hang in there a bit longer. Remember, this story is about my not being religious and how that relates to happiness. Nan and I were married 11 years before we had children. Our twins, Dave and Jen, were born in 1980. We sought out a Unitarian-Universalist Church. Most people seem to know little about Unitarianism and tend to see it as a cult or Johnny-Come-Lately sort of religion. Neither is the case. At the Unitarian Church, all religions are honored and are taught in the education program for the children. My mother-in-law attended Easter and Christmas with us. My mother came to the Passover and Chanukah services. My wife got very involved with the church. I never got as involved, opting to run road races most Sunday mornings. Okay, so you see that I've never been a regular church-goer or synagogue-goer or anything religious-goer, so I think you'll be interested to learn two things about me that nobody knows.

The first thing is that as a mid-life adult, I read the entire Bible cover to cover. Yes, every word. No, it was not an assignment. Yes, both the old and new testaments. No, not in one sitting. Yes, I'm glad I did it. No, I don't plan to do it again. Yes, I think it made a difference to me. No, I wouldn't recommend that you do it. What I did do is write down everything that had an impact on me in a little notebook that I continue to refer to decades later. I guess it's my mini-version of the Bible. But, I'm not religious. You should probably know that I've also read the Bhagavad-Gita, the I Ching, the Tao Te Ching, the Upanishads, the Kaballa, part of the Koran, and many other religious tomes. Curious? Yes. Religious? No.

The second thing that I want you to know about me is something that I may not have revealed to anyone up to this point in time. When you read this, try to suspend your judgment for a little while. Here it goes. I pray everyday for an hour. Having difficulty suspending your judgment? Have you labeled me as a religious fanatic? How about a nut job or an obsessive compulsive? Do you want to say to me, "Get a life!"? Have I lost credibility with regard to my not being religious? Give me a chance to explain.

Before you ask me where I find the time to pray an hour a day, let me ask you a few questions. If I decide to pray an hour daily instead of watching television for that hour, does that make me compulsive or fanatical? Many people can't seem to find the time to pray at length because they value watching a lot of TV. I find prayer to help me feel at peace and connected to the universe. It provides a meaningful and comforting ritual for me. It gives me an opportunity to express my gratitude and my concern for others and the world we share. I do not pray to win the lottery or for the Yankees to win the game. I pray for many things on many levels, but never for personal gain. I think praying is a healthy choice that I reinvest in on a daily basis. I don't only pray in difficult times. I take nothing for granted. Each day I wake is an opportunity for me to give thanks and feel connected.

Usually, I pray during my morning run. On those rare days when I don't run, I find other ways to get it in. Although I always try to be one-minded, praying is the one thing I allow myself to do while also doing other things. For example, I may pray in the shower or while getting ready for work. I allow myself that concession. To me, reading the holy books is educating myself so I can make my own decisions what to believe in and what not to. To me, praying is no guarantee of anything, but is a way of cultivating happiness by saying thank you for my being alive and able to experience this amazing existence.

I'm not suggesting that you pray an hour daily. I'm not suggesting you become more religious. My experience with religion leaves me ambivalent. At worst, religion is narrow minded and intolerant of individual differences, guilt provoking, highly judgmental, and leads to "holy" wars. At best, religion is, well, a religious experience. But the majority of my religious experiences have had little to do with religion. They've had more to do with awe, love, mystery, and transcending labels and categories.

So, that's why I am not religious, but I read books about it, pray faithfully, and believe that faith and belief in something larger than our individual selves is a key ingredient for happiness. I think religion is more about how we live our lives than what clergy tell us we should believe in.

A human being is part of a whole, the 'Universe.'
Our task must be to free ourselves from the delusion
of separateness; to embrace all living creatures
and the whole of nature.
-Albert Einstein

Dr. Jeckyl and Mr. Hyde

Most people are familiar with the story of Dr. Jeckyl and Mr. Hyde. The good compassionate doctor's own experimentation via injecting himself with a formula leads him to become a beastly, cruel, grotesque murderer. I find this to be a rather fascinating story because I can identify with it. It seems unnecessary to drink a potion or inject myself with a secret formula to realize I am both Jeckyl and Hyde.

Jeckyl is the part of me that wants to be liked, loved, do the right thing, and be a good human being. Hyde is the part of me that is selfish, wants what I want when I want it, and wants to satisfy my needs and impulses regardless of considering the consequences. I think there's a bit of Jeckyl and a bit of Hyde in each of us. There's nothing wrong with that. You can accept the Hyde in you even though you don't have to act upon those Hydean thoughts and inclinations. And, don't expect that you'll be Dr. Jeckyl all the time. That most likely will not happen.

My children will hopefully tell you that I'm a good, caring, fair, and loving father. I am certain they also can vividly relate episodes of my losing my temper and frightening them; of my being a very scary animal-like father figure. We can all laugh about it. The trick is to be Dr. Jeckyl most of the time, be aware of your Mr. Hyde side, and accept it while trying to minimize the times it is turned into action.

To some degree, we are all hiding Hydes. Don't let your Hyde fool you into thinking there's something wrong with you. You don't need a lobotomy or tranquilizers because you are a human being who sometimes has aggressive, selfish, or sexual thoughts or impulses. Don't be intimidated by your thoughts. They are "just thoughts" with no real influence unless you decide to plug into them emotionally or turn them into action. No need to deny or repress the Hyde in you, but do your best not to act on it. Happiness is connected to manifesting Dr. Jeckyl and just observing Mr. Hyde.

A Cherokee Elder was teaching his grandchildren about life. He said to them, "A fight is going on inside of me...it is a terrible fight between two wolves. One wolf represents fear, anger, envy, sorrow, regret, greed, arrogance, self-pity, guilt, resentment, inferiority, lies, false pride, and superiority. The other stands for joy, peace, love, hope, sharing, serenity, humility, kindness, benevolence, friendship, empathy, generosity, truth, compassion, and faith. This same fight is going on inside you, and inside every other person too."

They thought about it for a minute and then, one child asked his grandfather, "Which wolf will win?"

The old man simply replied, "The one you feed."

Honeymoon

I had been in the army about three months when I made the big decision. I would ask Nan to marry me. After all, we'd been dating over two and a half years and she was twenty years old. Yes, the Vietnam War was raging and I still had almost two years left of military service, but that knowledge didn't seem to present any obstacles as far as I was concerned. I was a private making $87 a month and was ready to settle down. I was a man with a plan.

At this point, I was stationed at a military hospital in El Paso, Texas. Nan lived with her family a couple of thousand miles away in Brooklyn, New York. I worked up the courage to phone her and propose. She excitedly said yes, but asked me to ask her father. He was 76 years old at the time and was a very conservative gentleman of very few words. Nan put him on the phone. I asked his permission to marry his daughter.

He asked, "How much longer will you be in the army?"

I replied, "About two years."

He queried, "How much money do you make?"

I answered, "$87 a month."

He then matter-of-factly stated, "After you're out of the army, and after you work a good job for a few years and save a lot of money, give me another call and we'll talk about it."

After overhearing the conversation, Nan, who was in her bathrobe at the time, began sobbing and ran out of the house. The police picked her up wandering around the neighborhood streets about a half hour later. They brought her home. We were married a few months later when I was able to get a week off. After the wedding, we had to get right back to the base, so there was no time for a honeymoon.

Feeling badly that I had uprooted this 20 year old girl from college and from her home, and that I brought her to a life in the desert replete with dust storms and tumbleweed, I decided that she should at least have a honeymoon, or something resembling

one. Once again, I was the man with a plan. I bought a book entitled, to the best of my recollection, *Mexico On Five Dollars a Day*.
We would travel from El Paso to Mexico City and, after spending a
few glorious days there, we would travel to Acapulco for a few more
days of serenity, fun, and sun. It would be a honeymoon to remember. Of course, we had to make some accommodations to be able
to do it on five dollars a day.

We did all the traveling by bus. It was not a luxury bus. No
air conditioning (despite it being Mexico in the summer). No bathroom. No one on the bus who spoke English. Chickens running
around. Did that really matter? We were only on that bus for 26
hours! It was quite an adventure. Our honeymoon. Nan was barely talking to me when we arrived in Mexico City.

In order to make it on the previously mentioned five dollars
a day, we were unable to stay at The Hilton, or Howard Johnson's,
or Motel 6, or any other place with a recognizable name. We stayed
at a little, rundown hotel in a non-Americanized section where no
one knew English. Despite neither of us knowing Spanish, the first
two days went fine. A bakery near our hotel sold fresh rolls for a
quarter per dozen (it was 36 years ago), so after rolls and coffee
and our room rent, we still had a few dollars left to get through the
day. We walked as much as we could and occasionally took a bus.
On day three, Nan got sick and we wound up spending the day in a
hospital. So, she was not particularly thrilled the next day when we
got on a bus for a seven hour ride to Acapulco. Queasy when we
arrived, we went to a small restaurant and ordered soup. The waiter ladled some out and a large fish head appeared in Nan's bowl.
One eye was staring at her. She excused herself from the table.

When it became apparent that this honeymoon stuff would
kill her, Nan became assertive. She may have only been 20 years
old and may have been sick to her stomach, but Nan had had
enough. She told me that we needed to fly back to El Paso when
we were finished in Acapulco. Although I knew that it would put a
crimp in our $5 a day honeymoon budget, I intuitively understood
that it would be important for me to acquiesce.

The last two days in Acapulco were great. Nan's illness
had run its course and we both relaxed and enjoyed. We laid in
hammocks on the beach and drank daiquiris while watching the
sun set. Yes, I had planned one heckuva honeymoon. What had
started out shaky finished just fine. Sometimes happiness takes a
circuitous route. Nan was resilient and experienced the eternal

truth that "this too shall pass." Resiliency and happiness go hand in hand. We had the perfect honeymoon. Even the muggers we escaped from on our final day there couldn't really dampen our spirits.

When you get to the end of your rope,
tie a knot and hang on.
-F.D.R.

Some Things Never Change

In *The Goddess and the Bull, Catalhoyuk: An Archaeological Journey to the Dawn of Civilization*, Michael Balter presents evidence explaining why humans first turned away from nomadic wandering and toward villages and togetherness. This fascinating account of Catalhoyuk, a 9,500 year old settlement in Turkey, describes one of the largest and best preserved Neolithic sites ever discovered. Before Catalhoyuk blossomed, the previous millennia was characterized by nomads who hunted game and gathered fruits and nuts and did not participate in communal living. But in Catalhoyuk, as many as 8,000 people laid down roots together and formed a community. It grew to be a very tight knit neighborhood. In fact, the buildings and houses were packed so closely together that those who lived there had to enter through the roofs.

Why did this move "from nomad to neighbors" occur? A hundred and twenty researchers from all over the globe have put their heads together from 1993 to the present to answer this question. Why is this even an important question?

> ...there's no doubt the Neolithic Revolution changed humanity forever. The roots of civilization were planted along with the first crops of wheat and barley, and it's not a stretch to say that the mightiest of today's skyscrapers can trace their heritage to the Neolithic architects who built the first stone dwellings. Nearly everything that came afterward, including organized religion, writing, cities, social inequality, population explosions, traffic jams, mobile phones, and the internet has roots in the moment people decided to live together in communities.
>
> -Michael Balter

And so it was that satisfying basic needs for food and shelter was not enough. Humans turned to villages and togetherness to meet the higher level needs of belongingness and love. The people of Catalhoyuk longed for culture, shared community, values, religion, and myth. They longed for meaning and purpose in life together and in death together. In this day and age, as families shrink and houses grow farther apart, technology makes it easier for us to be isolated or feel alienated. If that is the case for you, it is essential that you find ways to bring about a sense of belonging.

If you are living with too much isolation, you are going against the grain of what we know from research in the fields of archaeology, anthropology, sociology, paleoecology, and psychology. Abraham Maslow developed a hierarchy of needs that require satisfaction in order for a person to eventually feel fulfilled and truly happy. It turns out that it will be difficult for you to reach your potentials and to become self-actualized if you do not satisfy your need for belongingness. What Maslow means when he talks of self-actualization is a person who is positive in outlook, accepting of self and others, manifests a generosity of spirit and a good sense of humor, and who has satisfying relationships while functioning well independently. The self-actualized person feels loved and deeply appreciates life.

Sounds good, doesn't it? But you can't get there without that aforementioned sense of belongingness. That's the need that created communities. It could be belonging to a family, a spiritual group, a community group, or a support group. It could be belonging to a team or any group or interest that has a sub-culture attached to it. Find people that you can feel at home with and be yourself, without fear of ridicule or rejection. Life is difficult and the one thing we can be certain of is that everything changes. We need to hang together. Meet your needs for belongingness and you will be much happier. The people of Catalhoyuk knew that 9,500 years ago. Some things never change.

Reaching For the Starfish

I think that you greatly increase your chances of obtaining happiness if you regularly ask yourself two questions:

(1) What can I do?
(2) How can I help?

The famous neo-Freudian psychologist, Alfred Adler, advised all his unhappy and depressed patients to do something nice for others. It is a way of becoming less preoccupied with yourself. The others can be important people in your life or can even be strangers. A best-selling book this past decade had to do with performing "random acts of kindness." In either event, doing something nice for others or for the environment will help lift your spirits and produce feelings of self-gratification. Try it. Then, try it again. Try it regularly. Do what I refer to as a 30-30. Do one nice thing everyday for 30 consecutive days. You may be surprised at the impact this can have on how you feel. And can you imagine how the world would change if everybody did that?

Mother Teresa said, "Do not wait for the leaders. Do it alone, person to person." She was talking about helping out, taking action. Mahatma Gandhi urged, "Be the change that you want to see in the world." There are countless ways that you can help. You can get unstuck from dwelling on your unhappiness by answering the two questions I posed at the outset of this story. Doing so will help satisfy your need to be appreciated and to make a difference.

The Zen Monk, Ryokan, was walking by the sea where the tide had washed ashore many hundreds of starfish. They would soon die of exposure. Ryokan was slowly picking up the starfish, one at a time, and tossing them back into the ocean.

A Zen student, Saito, was witnessing the event. "Why do you bother?" Saito asked Ryokan, overwhelmed by the sheer number of starfish dying. "It won't make any difference."

Ryokan stopped for a moment, looking at the starfish in his hand. He replied, "It will to this one."

In *After the Ecstasy, the Laundry*, Jack Kornfield quotes Mother Teresa:

I never look at the masses as my responsibility; I look at the individual. I can only love one person at a time – just one, one, one. So you begin. I began – I picked up one person. Maybe if I didn't pick up that one person, I wouldn't have picked up forty-two thousand. The whole work is only a drop in the ocean. But if I didn't put the drop in, the ocean would be one drop less. The same thing goes for you, the same thing in your family, the same thing in your church, your community. Just begin – one, one, one.

You probably think about how to help and what you can do. You may even talk about it. It's important that you do it.

Happiness is when what you think,
what you say, and what you do
are in harmony.
-Mahatma Gandhi

The Struggle

This book has repeatedly stated that we all know that life is difficult. At times, it can be quite a struggle. It's the nature of the beast, as it were. And struggles are an inevitable and necessary part of life.

A man found a cocoon of a butterfly. One day a small opening appeared. He sat and watched the butterfly for several hours as it struggled to force its body through that little hole. It seemed to stop making any progress. It appeared as if it had gotten as far as it could and that it could go no farther.

The man decided to help the butterfly, so he took a pair of scissors and snipped off the remainder of the cocoon. The butterfly then emerged easily. But it had a swollen body and small, shriveled wings. The man continued to watch the butterfly because he expected that, at any moment, the wings would enlarge and expand to be able to support the body, which would contract in time.

Neither happened! In fact, the butterfly spent the rest of its life crawling around with a swollen body and shriveled wings. It never was able to fly. What the man in his kindness and haste had not understood was that the restricting cocoon and the struggle required for the butterfly to get through the tiny opening were nature's way of forcing fluid from the body of the butterfly into its wings. In this manner, it would be ready for flight once it achieved its freedom from the cocoon.

Sometimes struggles are exactly what we need in our life. If nature allowed us to go through our life without any obstacles, it would cripple us. We would not be as strong as what we could have been.

And we could never fly...

-Author unknown

The Happiness Solution

Daniel Gilbert, a psychology professor at Harvard, studies happiness. When people ask him why he studies happiness, he replies, "Why study anything else? It's the holy grail. We're studying the thing that all human action is directed toward." Gilbert's research concludes that we overestimate the intensity and duration of how we'll respond emotionally to events that happen to us. With both positive and negative events, Gilbert says, "You're overestimating how much of a difference they make. None of them make the difference you think." With regard to negative events and struggles, his findings suggest that we are much more resilient than we believe we are. We bounce back and continue to strive for and find happiness, joy, and meaning. He wants us to know that we are just lousy predictors when we are in the midst of grappling with difficult situations. Our predictions of how terrible we'll always feel are off the mark. Struggles typically will neither kill us or relegate us to a doom and gloom future.

Don't Believe Everything You Think
-Bumper sticker

In due time, we all have our fair share of struggling and suffering. Buddha said that we suffer because we want things to be different than they are. But things are as they are. Always and in all ways. We're always surrounded by truth. Even lies are truth, if you know what I mean.

If you think you have suffered more than others and are more entitled to complain, visit the Tree of Sorrows. You may be very surprised. I think one of the worst things that could happen to someone is to lose a child. At the Tree of Sorrows, there will be people who've lost two, three, or more children. Every person is allowed to hang his or her unhappiness, struggles, and sufferings on a branch of the gigantic Tree of Sorrows. After all have found a limb from which their miseries may dangle, you may walk slowly around the tree and search for a set of sufferings that you'd prefer instead of the set you hung on the tree. The likelihood is that you will reclaim your own assortment of struggles and sufferings rather than those of another. And, you'll probably leave the Tree of Sorrows a bit wiser than when you arrived.

Try to cultivate the belief that whatever comes your way, you'll be able to deal with it and cope with it. It's true, and believing it may help you feel a little more secure and a little happier as well.

Baba Yaga

She lives deep within a forest in the center of the earth. Her hut stands on large chicken legs, spins, and emits blood curdling screeches, creaking, and groaning. The hut is surrounded by a fence made of bones. The fence is topped with skulls. The skulls have blazing eye sockets that stand out amidst the pitch blackness. She is Baba Yaga and is portrayed vividly in Russian, Slavic, and Hungarian folk tales.

Baba Yaga is the archetypal hag, the old witch, the crone, and the untamable Bone Mother. Despite her horrifying appearance, she is also the Earth Mother and possesses the power of nature and all the seasons. She is terrifying but also has answers to the secrets of life and death. Baba Yaga is a guardian between the world of mortals and the world of spirits. She is a reflection of your shadow. She is Darth Vader but is also Yoda. In Russian folk tales, Baba Yaga sits in the dark and eats.

When visitors enter her hut (which seldom happens), Baba Yaga asks them whether they came of their own free will, or whether they were sent. Only one answer is right. Legend has it that she helps the pure of heart and eats the souls of those who visit her unprepared and unclean of spirit. For those who are willing to face her and dare to ask, she'll provide answers and compassion. If you offer her the dark parts of yourself, she will eat them and help you to understand and accept all of you as you transform and transcend. Give her all you have in the dark recesses of your psyche. As you sit with Baba Yaga again and again, you will become less fearful and more trusting and accepting of yourself and the universe.

As children, we tease by saying, "She's afraid of her own shadow," and we break out in laughter. As adults, we may be afraid of our own shadows in a very different way. In a way, facing Baba Yaga is like facing the Baba Yaga in yourself. People deemed to possess the character strengths of curiosity, honesty, and courage are more likely to be happy. These are also the traits necessary to deal with Baba Yaga. As frightening as Baba Yaga is to come face to face with, she wants you to understand that there is "nothing to be afraid of." Is this the ultimate reassurance or the ultimate terror, or both?

Remember the firefighters who were running into the World Trade Center as everyone was running out? Dr. Dan Baker writes of them:

> It's a perfect metaphor for the kind of people we all need to be, if we're ever going to be truly happy. We need to be willing to charge headlong into the inferno of our most horrific fears – eyes open, intellect and spirit at the ready – even as our survival instincts are screaming, 'Run! Run! Get out!'

Look Baba Yaga in the eye. That's what William Tell did. Read about it in the next story.

"This Is the Spot"

In a recent issue of *Smithsonian*, the prolific Robert Wernick begins his article on William Tell with the following passage:

> In the center of the town square stands a heroic bronze figure, a stern, sturdy, bearded man in homespun clothes, crossbow over his shoulder, his arm around a barefooted boy. Before him stands another stern, sturdy man, this one in a neat business suit, respectfully silent, with his arm around another small boy, this one wearing Reebok running shoes. The man points to the ground. "This," he tells the boy, "is the spot."

The spot refers to the birthplace of Switzerland. Legend has it that in the year 1307, in the mountains of Uri, and in the busy market square of Altdorf, an event took place that would literally shape a nation. Wernick provides the following account, which I've paraphrased: Bailiff Gessler, an agent of the Hapsburg Duke of Austria, boldly placed a Hapsburg hat on a pole and, with trumpets blaring, declared that all those walking by must remove their hats to pay honor to the powerful Hapsburg empire. A local Uri farmer and hunter, William Tell, entered the town square with his young son.

Tell kept his hat on his head. He was immediately dragged to the bailiff. Gessler ordered that an apple be placed on the head of Tell's son. William was informed that he had to shoot the apple off the boy's head with a single arrow, at a distance of 120 paces. If he was unsuccessful in this task, both he and the boy would be put to death. Tell put two arrows in his jacket. He then paced off the distance, loaded and armed his crossbow. He shot his arrow. It hit its mark and the apple fell to the ground. Gessler said, "Your life is now safe, but kindly tell me why I saw you putting a second arrow inside your jacket?"

Tell replied, "If my first arrow had killed my son, I would have shot the second at you, and I would not have missed." The furious Gessler ordered that Tell be tied up and carried to a boat on Lake Lucerne, which would take him to a dungeon in the sinister castle of Kussnacht. There, he was going to spend the rest of his life and "nevermore see sun or moon." A ferocious wind jeopardized the safety of all the boat's passengers. Tell was the only one aboard with the strength to steer the boat to safety, so he was freed from bondage. When he got close to a large, flat rock by the water's edge, Tell leapt ashore and, with a swift and powerful kick, sent Gessler and his loyalists back into the violent water.

Tell did not underestimate the wrath and determination of Gessler and his men. He believed they would make it to shore. Therefore, Tell negotiated 20 miles of dark woods and mountain trails to the Hohle Gasse, a narrow pass that lead to Kussnacht. Tell hid behind a tree, waiting for Gessler. He used that oft mentioned second arrow and shot Gessler dead. Later, Tell met with three other men in a forest meadow that eventually became known as Rutli. This was the start of a movement of national liberation. The Swiss Federation, which is still going strong today, had its beginning when a local man, William Tell, looked the Hapsburg empire squarely in the eye and did not blink.

There is much more of the tale of William Tell, but I have told the part of it that I think is important for you to know. Whether the tale is fact or fiction or embellished misses the point. So, what is the point? I would say it's that a solitary person's actions can make an incredible difference. Many people feel a sense of impotency, as if their lives don't matter. Standing up for something you strongly believe in can help you feel significantly better. Empower yourself with self-respect. Pull a William Tell. It doesn't have to be as dramatic as Tell's actions. Your day to day decisions to act courageously, even in little ways, will have you feeling happier about yourself.

And they came for the Tibetan Buddhists,
and I didn't protest.
And they came for the Muslims,
and I didn't protest.
And they came for the Hindus,
and I didn't protest.
And they came for the American Indians,

and I didn't protest.
And they came for the Asian Americans,
and I didn't protest.
And they came for the African Americans,
and I didn't protest.
And they came for the Jews,
and I didn't protest.
And they came for the Mormons,
and I didn't protest.
And they came for the Jehovah's Witnesses,
and I didn't protest.
And they came for the 7th Day Adventists,
and I didn't protest.
And they came for the Catholics,
and I didn't protest.
And they came for the Protestants,
and I didn't protest.
And they came for the Christians,
and I didn't protest.
And they came for the Atheists,
and I didn't protest.
And they came for me,
and there was no one left to protest.

-Homage to Martin Niemoller

Four In a Fiat

When we were all in our 20's, my wife, Nan, and I, and our friends, Tony and Sherry, traveled through Europe. Tony and I were roommates in college where we dated Sherry and Nan. We married about a year apart. Tony and I had recently finished a couple of years in the army and we were getting our careers started. We figured it would be a good time to do some traveling.

In Rome, we rented a tiny red Fiat (it looked like it should have come with a wind-up mechanism) to set out for a town called Bergamo. Sherry had relatives there and wanted to pay a visit. Somewhere in the Alps, we got lost. Despite being four reasonably intelligent human beings, we were unable to get anywhere near the vicinity of Bergamo. The more we tried, the more lost we got. We were exhausting the daylight but were no closer to finding our way out of the Alps. Nightfall found us sooner than later. We were hungry, tired, and losing visibility in the mountain fog. There were no other people in the area and no other cars traveling through. We were alone, lost, and could no longer even see the mountain road we'd been traversing. Having almost zero visibility, Tony slowly pulled off the road. This was before the cell phone era. We were surrounded by blackness.

We got out of the car but couldn't see anything. We had neither a flashlight nor a flare. It was cold and getting colder. We were scared, but at that point, our trembling had more to do with the cold than our fright. We knew we were somewhere high in the Italian Alps and that we were stranded on the side of the road, but that's about all we knew at that point. We got back into the undersized fiat. Sherry and Nan were in the back, with Tony and I up front. Being that it was hot and sunny that morning, we all left without coats since it was only supposed to be a day trip. High in the Alps that night we were very cold and shivered throughout. We felt like sardines in a can. There was no room to spread out or stretch. Comments like, "Could you please get your elbow out of my ear?" occurred regularly.

We did manage to get some sleep. The morning mist and fog began to dissipate and visibility was slowly being restored. Sunrise brought with it two astonishing views. The first was a near-by glistening, snow-capped mountain peak. The second was the view of where our car was parked. It was at the very edge of the road, about a foot from going over the side of the mountain. There was no guardrail. In the darkness of the night, if Tony had driven one or two feet more as he was pulling off the road, we would have dropped off the mountain to our certain deaths. Nan and Sherry began crying when they realized how close we had come to dying. We were all shaken. We began driving down the mountain. Eventually we came to a populated area and there was a small restaurant in a house. We knocked on the door. It was about 6:30 in the morning and the restaurant was closed. The owners, who lived there, opened up and listened to our story. They made us coffee and gave us directions.

We never did get to Bergamo. We did make it back and we were able to laugh about the whole thing. In fact, 35 years later, we look at Tony and Sherry's slides from that Europe trip and we roar hysterically. Did we really dress that way and think we were cool? Did we really go there? And, look at that Fiat. Unbelievable.

The trip to Bergamo was a lot like life. There was uncertainty and adventure. We never counted on getting lost and didn't anticipate all those twists and turns. At times we had little idea where we were going or how it would turn out. It was scary and fun. We started out hopeful, lost our way, got discouraged, endured, and found our way. We bonded, met nice people, and were moved to tears when we realized the full scope of our predicament and fate. We were on the precipice and we not only survived but later thrived. Life is like that. A really happy person is one who's capable of enjoying the scenery on a detour.

Wabi-Sabi

Wabi-Sabi is a Zen-inspired recognition of the beauty of things that are imperfect, impermanent, and incomplete. It embraces the rustic and can be traced back to the first Japanese teahouse that was designed in the 16th century by the Tea Master, Sen no Rikyo. Waba-Sabi is an aesthetic dealing with things that are deteriorating, decomposing, decaying, used, worn, or irregular. The opposite of Wabi-Sabi would include new, shiny, slick, symmetrical, uniform, designer, and modern. Wabi-Sabi items tell a story.

In the early 1990's, Leonard Koren, an architectural writer living in Japan, was photographing the progression of decaying leaves. It lead him to write a book about the centuries old concept of Wabi-Sabi. The book, *Wabi-Sabi For Artists, Designers, Poets, and Philosophers*, was published in 1994 and has slowly made its way to the Western World. In a recent interview, Koren said:

> I think Wabi-Sabi's greatest appeal is that it's the absolute antithesis of classical Western beauty. Whereas the beauty that we inherited from the Greeks and Romans is monumental, enduring, gorgeous, grand, and powerful, Wabi-Sabi is a beauty of the exact opposite.
>
> ...Wabi-Sabi is an antidote to an over saturation of cars, slick computers, digital this, and digital that.

One of my hobbies is photographing old wooden items that reveal an unmistakable passage of time. The wood has devolved in a natural way. It's raw and unembellished. I've shot a lot of barns and even a few outhouses. A variety of buoys, timeworn crates, and an interesting lobster shack. Years ago, running at dawn on a deserted, foggy beach, I came across an extremely weathered Adirondack chair that almost blended right into the grey, misty morning. I dashed home for my camera and took a photo. The picture of that chair is part of my collection of Wabi-Sabi art.

Wabi-Sabi is also a philosophy of simplicity and parsimony. It is not interested in adding anything symbolic or unnecessary. It's like haiku poetry. It's neither chic nor fashionable, but rather earthy and unpretentious.

> pier sunset
> in old wooden baskets
> crabs crawl on crabs

Inherent in Wabi-Sabi is an appreciation of the cosmic order and an acceptance of the inevitable. As things devolve from and toward nothingness, Wabi-Sabi teaches us that truth comes from observing nature and that we need to come to terms with our own Wabi-Sabi existence.

Here's our predicament. We live in a society that values youth and devalues age. Newer and sleeker and younger are desirable. That's the anti-Wabi-Sabi mantra continually being chanted by advertising media. Did I say "being chanted?" Make that "being shoved down our throats." If you are old, listen to this advice. Actually, even if you're not old, take heed, for you will hopefully be old someday also. By the way, my definition of old is anyone who's at least ten years older than me, regardless of how old I am. Here's the advice. Do not accept invitations to feel useless or as if you have nothing left to offer. Remember Wabi-Sabi. There is beauty and wisdom in the natural aging process and in things imperfect and impermanent.

> The older the fiddler,
> the sweeter the tune.
> -English Proverb

Some of the psychotherapy sessions I look most forward to are with my clients who are in their late 70's, 80's, and 90's. I don't mind making house calls and I continue to learn about aging through our meetings. For the most part, they are much less concerned with death than those who are much younger than them. Research bears this out. Young adults and middle aged people are not happier than our senior population. Older people seem to be able to live more in the moment and not get too far ahead of themselves. And they still feel like kids inside and evidence playfulness and delightful senses of humor. I find old people to be like

Wabi-Sabi art. They're rough around the edges, asymmetrical, and have been decomposing for quite awhile. They have their own beauty, a beauty of imperfection and acceptance of it.

So, don't think old age is nothing to look forward to. It may be hard. It may not be a picnic. But you can be happy, and in some ways, it might bring you more contentment and peace-of-mind than at other times in your life. Think Wabi-Sabi. If I have to die, and I'm given the choice as to what to die from, I'll choose old age.

What Were You Thinking?

In mythology, there is a fire-breathing she-monster represented as having a lion's head, a goat's body, and a serpent's tail.
This monster is Chimera. A chimera (small 'c') has come to be
known as a mental fabrication or a grotesque product of the imag-
ination. Without realizing it, people are producing chimeras day in
and day out. When patients tell me they are feeling anxiety or depression, I typically ask them what they've been thinking about, or,
what they've been telling themselves. I often think that if I told
myself all day long what they tell themselves, I'd be anxious and
depressed also.

In *The Art of Happiness*, the Dalai Lama discusses how our
happiness or lack of it is related to our thought processes. It ties in
neatly with current psychotherapeutic technique in the western
world. The Dalai Lama writes, "...our positive states of mind can
act as antidotes to our negative tendencies and delusory states of
mind." He urges that those suffering from negative emotional states
should apply antidotes such as patience, tolerance, kindness, love,
compassion, forgiveness, and doing nice things for others. Unlike
Freud who believed that the innate selfish drives of humans are
instinctual, the Dalai Lama's "method for achieving happiness is
based on the revolutionary idea that negative mental states are
not an intrinsic part of our minds; they are transient obstacles that
obstruct the expression of our underlying natural state of joy and
happiness."

The method of training the mind to let go of negativity by
seeking positive states of mind as antidotes is somewhat akin to
cognitive behavioral therapy (CBT). The basis of CBT is that our
negative emotions (anxiety, depression, etc.) and maladaptive behaviors are a result of distortions in thinking and irrational beliefs.
Therapy focuses on the identification and correction of those distortions. In other words, your unhappiness is related to distorted

thought patterns, and correcting those distortions is the antidote that does away with the unhappiness.

A study of Chinese Americans confirms that what you think can be a matter of life and death. Two beliefs were looked at. The first belief is that a person's fate is determined by the astrological year of his or her birth (i.e. the year of the monkey). The second is that each astrological year is associated with a type of illness. In a recent issue of *American Psychologist*, Dr. Oakley Ray summarized the study:

> When a believer in these concepts develops the illness associated with his or her birth year, that person believes that his or her belief system has been confirmed and that an early death is probable. This study asked the simple question, 'When an individual committed to this astrological system develops an illness that is associated with his or her birth year, does that person die sooner than individuals with the same illness who were born in a different astrological year or who have a lesser commitment to the belief system?'

The evidence was indisputable. Yes, such people do die sooner. That belief system shortened believer's lives by up to five years. You've heard the old axiom, "You are what you eat." Well, it's not a stretch to state, "You are what you think." Recent well-designed longitudinal research studies have confirmed that your thoughts and attitude can add as much as eight years to your life. Are you feeding yourself toxic or nourishing thoughts? Changing your diet of thoughts could add years to your life and happiness to your years.

Up the Ante

I've been running regularly for almost forty years. Mostly I run by myself. It's just part of my day. An important part. I guess you could say I'm passionate about running. Once, I asked myself the question, "If you were the only person left in the world, would you continue to run?" The answer came instantly. "Of course." I'm a runner. That's part of how I define myself. I run on roads, on treadmills, on trails, tracks, and well, just about wherever I can. The weather typically doesn't matter. I dress for it.

As a child and teenager, I was an extremely slow runner. You know how a very tall guy might be given the nickname "Shorty?" My nickname was "Lightening." Once I hit a line drive that the right fielder picked up on one bounce and proceeded to throw me out at first base. I was a bit bottom heavy and, despite being a good athlete, I was teased repeatedly by my friends and teammates. In my twenties, I dropped about 50 pounds and realized I could run a bit faster and maintain it. I was no longer "the slow guy." I ran local road races and major marathons. Maybe I was compensating for my early history, repairing the embarrassment of teenage teasing and the like. Regardless of why I became passionate about running, the important thing is that I did. Passion is a lifeline to happiness. It's not enough in and of itself, but the capacity to live passionately is enormously important. Tap into that part of you that wants to live as good and as meaningful and as joyous a life as you possibly can. Passion breeds zest and enthusiasm, traits found to be highly correlated with satisfaction, happiness, and living the good life.

This year I realized that I was slowing down. My workouts at the high school track felt a bit different. My 5-K road race times got slower. Despite varying attempts to train more diligently, my times remained slower. I'm not sure why I did what I did, but I decided to up the ante and go for it. I saw a flyer for an event called the Mountain Man Biathlon. Here's what it said: "This more than challenging biathlon is complete with mud, sweat, bad weather, mountainous trails, and leg burning climbs. Terrain is off-road with rocks and logs and mud and streams and bones of dead animals."

I knew immediately that I wanted to try it. With some measure of trepidation, I set out that crisp October morning, not fully knowing how I'd respond to the challenging mountain biking and running. Despite falling off the bike once and falling twice during the runs, I finished, albeit a bit battered and bruised. I felt good. Okay, if the truth be known, I felt great. Alive. Restored. Regenerated. I had upped the ante. Poked the embers. Stirred the pot. I thought of George Santayana, the philosopher who said, "Never have I enjoyed youth so much as in my old age."

I want you to consider upping the ante. I'm not necessarily talking about anything related to exercise, running, or physical activity, although that is one possible route to take. Upping the ante can be challenging yourself in any way that's meaningful for you. You can up the ante intellectually. Learn something new. You can up the ante spiritually. You can up it at work, at home, or anywhere in any way. It is the opposite of resting on your laurels. It's the opposite of stagnation. It's not about playing it safe and having instant replay over and over. It's about finding the passion within you and discovering new arenas and new solutions to existing situations that have grown stale. Up the ante and you'll up your happiness quotient.

Albert Einstein was visited one day by one of his students.

"The questions on this year's exam are the same as last year's!" the young man exclaimed.

"Yes," Einstein replied, "but this year all the answers are different."

The Chosen Ones

Maureen Dowd recently wrote an op-ed column in *The New York Times* that drew a parallel between President Clinton's behavior with Monica Lewinsky and President George W. Bush's declaration of war on Iraq. The common denominator was that they did it "because they could." Her point was that they acted based on arrogance without fully considering the consequences of their actions. Essentially, they did what they wanted to do. In fact, Clinton told Dan Rather, "I did something for the worst possible reason. Just because I could." He added, "I think that's just about the most morally indefensible reason anybody could have for doing anything."

There's a little post office next to the building where I've maintained my private practice for the past 27 years. It has three parking spots in front of it. I can see them from my office window. One of them is designated for handicapped parking. No doubt about it. Bright yellow lines, a prominent sign, and the universal symbol for handicapped parking painted in the middle of the spot all take the guesswork out of the equation. Indeed, it's a no-brainer. The images aren't even faded. No ambiguity here. All of this by way of saying it is most obvious that this is a spot for handicapped parking.

Today, a 30-something woman in a large, black SUV, parked in that spot that is not designated for the able bodied. She spryly got out of the car and went inside the post office. She appeared to have no afflictions that would entitle her to that parking space. Nothing on her car or license plates suggested she had official handicapped status. While she was inside the post office, a River Edge police car pulled behind her car so that she would be unable to drive in any direction. No escape was possible. After the obligatory license and registration routine, he began to write her a ticket. From my window, I could see she was very upset as she argued and dramatically gestured to help her make her case. I wondered what she could possibly be saying in her defense. She was parking

179

in a space she was not supposed to occupy. She got a ticket and then got angry at the officer for giving it to her. Am I missing something here?

This scenario is repeated throughout the day again and again. And it all takes place in one little parking space outside a very small post office that my office window happens to overlook. I imagine this event takes place every minute of every day somewhere in our country.

The arrogance connected to having a sense of entitlement almost assuredly leads to anger, frustration, and unhappiness. If you believe that you're entitled to do whatever you want (just because you can), you should know that there will be a price to pay for adopting that egocentric stance. You'll never truly be happy if you see yourself as a victim, i.e., the poor misunderstood housewife who was in a hurry to pick up her kids from school, so she quickly parked in the handicapped spot for only a minute, and that jerk of a cop gave her a ticket.

Take responsibility. For example, "I parked in the space I wasn't supposed to. I thought I'd get away with it. Well, I didn't. I got caught. I deserved a ticket. I won't do it again." You'll be happier. This way you'll realize that the policeman didn't cause your unhappiness – you did, by acting arrogantly. Treat yourself and everyone else (including the physically challenged) with respect by doing the right thing. Remember that golden oldie. Yes, I'm talking about the golden rule. "Do unto others all that you would have them do unto you..." is the Christian teaching appearing in the *Bible*. All religions seem to have a version of this in their respective holy books:

* Buddhism
    - Do not offend others as you would not wish to be offended.
* Confucianism
    - Is there a maxim that one ought to follow all his life? Surely the maxim of peaceful goodness: What we don't want done to us we should not do to others.
* Hinduism
    - All your duties are included in this: Do nothing to others that would pain you if it were done to you.

* Islam
  - No one of you will be a true believer who does not wish for his brother the same that he wishes for himself.
* Judaism
  - What you don't wish for yourself, do not wish for your neighbor. This is all the law, the rest is only commentary.
* Taoism
  - Hold as your own the gains of your neighbor and as yours his losses.

So here we are back at that post office parking spot. I wonder how the woman who got the ticket would feel if someone she didn't know parked in her spot in her driveway or in her garage? I'm guessing that she may have felt outraged and violated, thinking, "That person has no business being in my spot!" Hmmmmm. So to summarize, she parked in that post office spot because she could. It was there for the taking.

Narcissism, selfishness, and flaunting power plays inevitably all lead to unhappiness because they display an attitude of "I'm above you. I'm smarter. I'm better looking. I have more money than you. You're less than me." People will get the message and treat you accordingly. Pride, hubris, selfishness, and wealth will not buy you happiness. Treating others well and with respect may help.

We share a community and a world. If you throw your paper cup out the car window, you're littering OUR neighborhood. We're all in this together. We're all in the same boat, so to speak, but sometimes we all shouldn't be in the same parking space.

To Be or Not to Be

I recently received an unsolicited magazine called *Geezer-Jock*. It is geared towards Masters level athletes (age 40 and over) and has stories about track meets, training techniques, nutrition, travel, and various other items of interest to those competing in Masters level events. Going to a high-level Masters athletic event can be quite an eye opener. A couple of years ago, a filmmaker named Bill Haney went to the National Masters Track and Field Championships in Boston. He was there to simply cheer on a friend. He was stunned by what he saw. Amazed by the performances of people in their 40's, 50's, 60's, 70's, 80's, and 90's, and taken aback by their heartwarming and inspiring stories and personalities, he decided to make a documentary about some of the athletes. Aptly entitled *Racing Against the Clock*, it is testimony to the idea that "the human spirit doesn't decay."

In reading the letters to the editor section of *GeezerJock*, there were 22 letters dealing with the name of the magazine. Many readers found it "insulting" and "offensive," while others found it to be "disrespectful" and "obscure," and some even cancelled their subscriptions. They took offense to the geezer reference, feeling that it diminished their efforts and achievements. They suggested changing the name of the publication to *MasterSports*, *MasterAthlete*, or *Sports4Seniors*. I showed the issue I received to a good friend of mine. He hated the name. Even my wife didn't care for the idea that I was being referred to as a geezer.

I have to admit that I didn't mind the name at all. I thought it was kind of funny. And way before that magazine ever appeared, I'd survey the road races I was about to run for "the other geezers" that may have showed up that day. So I had already placed myself in the geezer category long before the magazine stereotyped me. I think it's more important to be able to make fun of yourself and to see the humor in things than it is to aggressively get on the defensive to protect some unrealistic image of yourself that denies and defies the fact that you're getting up there. Okay, maybe you can run a fast mile at age 63. Congratulations. But maybe you'd be a bit more relaxed and a bit happier if you'd get less bent out of shape over little things. Hey, part of me would also like to deny the inevitable of getting closer to hanging up the spikes. I'm reminded of my friend and colleague, Dr. Joseph Luciani, and his epitaph to be. Anyone visiting his gravesite will see the following tombstone:

I'd rather be reading this.
-Dr. Joe

Maybe I'm being a little too hard on the anti-geezer people. I understand where they're coming from. And I welcome their opinions and feelings about it. It makes it all a bit more interesting. Time is going quickly and if we can hold out from being classified as a geezer, maybe we'll feel as if we've slowed down the clock rather than as if we're racing against it. Isaac Asimov said:

Life is pleasant,
Death is peaceful.
It's the transition that's troubling.

Another esteemed friend and colleague of mind, Dr. Sam Menahem, a distinguished professor at Columbia, would evoke the words of one of his heroes, Groucho Marx:

Time flies like an arrow.
Fruit flies like a banana.

(You may have to read that one twice.)

Hey, we know that we're not geezers but we also know that we are. The joke is on us and that's fine. In 2003, the Harley Davidson Co. celebrated 100 years of selling motorcycles. The average age of a first time buyer of a Harley is now almost 50 years old. On Memorial Day, I saw a group of about 40 people riding their motorcycles on the highway. They were not spring chickens. They looked a pinch like leftover hippies from the 60's, and many of them appeared to be in their 60's. I smiled. I waved. I felt good. And Louis Armstrong was singing on the radio:

The Happiness Solution

...the bright blessed day,
the dark sacred night.
And I think to myself,
what a wonderful world.

I turned up the volume.

Coyote

I think it would be shortsighted to write a book on happiness without dealing with the issue of death. The next few stories will touch upon this. Many people fear their own deaths and the deaths of loved ones. It's natural to some degree, but if we obsess about it, we're in trouble. We need to move toward acceptance of life, which includes birth, infancy, youth, adulthood, middle age, old age, and death. And, maybe rebirth. Our culture's fascination with youth perpetuates our fears of aging and dying. Other cultures seem to have less of a problem.

In *Parabola*, a journal devoted to myth and the quest for meaning, we see how death is accepted and incorporated into other cultures:

For the Ndembu, death doesn't have the note of finality that it possesses in much of Western civilization. To die is the equivalent of reaching the end of a stage of development, a cycle of growth. After death, a person continues to be active, either as an ancestral spirit who watches the behavior of his living kin and may become manifest through various afflictions, or as partially reincarnated in a kinsman who demonstrates some of his mental and physical characteristics. So death is not thought of as an annihilation but rather as a change in social status, a different mode of existence.

For the Yaqui and Mayo Indians of Northwestern Mexico, the dead are regarded as continuing members of the family. They may intercede with saints and deities on behalf of the family. Books of the names of the dead family members are kept on the household altar, and these names are recited in prayers that include a special prayer for those whose names have been forgotten. To some extent, newly born children are regarded as reincarnated ancestors, establishing a continuous cycle of birth, death, and rebirth.

Maybe we need to work on taking death a little less seriously. Really, what are our choices? Even if we continually worry about it, that doesn't stave it off. There is no escape. No place to hide.

A man is walking in his village. He sees Death coming toward him. Deathly afraid, so to speak, the man flees as fast as he can. He arrives at another village and breathes a sign of relief. Suddenly, Death appears and grabs him and says, "Come."

The man says, "But Death, I saw you coming toward me in my village, so I fled here."

Death answers, "Yes, I was surprised to see you in your village because I knew I was to pick you up here in such a short time."

-Sufi Story

In his book *The Old Ways*, Gary Snyder relates American Indian myths having to do with Coyote, the multifaceted trickster who's always stirring the pot somewhere. He explains why there's death in the world:

Like it's Coyote's fault that there's death in the world. This from California, Maidu. Earthmaker made the world so that people wouldn't get old, wouldn't die. He made a lake so that if people began to feel as if they were getting old, they'd go get in this lake and get young again, and he made it so that every morning when you wake up, you reach outside your lodge and there's a cooked bowl, cooked mind you, of hot steaming acorn mush to eat. Didn't have to work for food in those days. Nobody died, and there was plenty of food, you just reached outside the door every morning, and there's some nice hot acorn mush. But Coyote went around agitating the human beings, saying, "Now, you folks, don't you think this is kind of a dull life, there ought to be something happening here, maybe you ought to die." And they'd say, "What's that, death?" And he'd say, "Well, you know, if you die, then you really have to take life seriously, you have to think about things more." And he kept agitating this way, and Earthmaker heard him agitating this way, and Earthmaker shook his head and said, "Oh boy, things are going to go all wrong now." So Coyote kept agitating his death idea around, and pretty soon things started happening. They were having a foot race, and Coyote's son was running in the foot race. Coyote

Man's son got out there, and by golly, he stepped on a rattlesnake and the rattlesnake bit him, and he fell over and lay on the ground, and everybody thought he was asleep for the longest time. Coyote kept shouting, "Wake up, come on now, run." Finally Earthmaker looked at him and said, "You know what happened? He's dead. You asked for it." And Coyote said, "Well, I changed my mind, I don't want people to die after all, now let's have him come back to life." But Earthmaker said, "It's too late now, it's too late now."

So there you have it. It's Coyote's fault. But, for Coyote, it's never the end of the line. There's always another story:

When Coyote went to the world above this one, the only way back was to come down a spider web, and the spider told him, "Now, when you go down that spider web, don't look down, and don't look back, just keep your eyes closed until your feet hit the bottom, and then you'll be okay." So he's going down this spider web, and he's gettin' kind of restless, and he says, "Well, now, I'm just sure I'm about to touch bottom now, any minute my foot's going to touch bottom, I'm going to open my eyes." And he opens his eyes, and naturally the spider web breaks, and he falls and kills himself. So he lies there, and the carrion beetles come and eat him, and some of his hair blows away and pretty soon his ribs are coming out. About six months go by and he really is looking messy, but he begins to wake up and opens one eye and the other, and he can't find the other eye, so he reaches out and sticks a pebble in his eye socket, and then a blue jay comes along and puts a little pine pitch on the pebble, and then he can see through that. And he sort of pulls himself back together and goes around and looks for a couple of his ribs that have kind of drifted down the hill, and pulls himself back together and says, "Well, now I'm going to keep on traveling."

Coyote is never surprised by anything. He deals with what comes his way. If he falls apart, he puts himself together again and looks forward to getting into some more mischief. Coyote is happy. He travels light. He sees life as an adventure. Life doesn't surprise him. Death doesn't surprise him. Afterlife doesn't surprise him. He looks life in the eye and he looks death in the eye. And he keeps on traveling.

The Verizon Store

We all have important events in our lives that we look forward to. Some are special, such as the graduation party or the summer vacation. These come along every now and again. Others are more regular, such as our Thursday night TV programs, our late night snacks, or meeting a friend for lunch. But most of the things that comprise our reality are not things we put on our calendars or eagerly await. It's as if they are "filler" moments. These "in-between" moments fill up our lives but we don't value them.

Driving to work, standing in line at the bank or supermarket, talking to a clerk, or filling the car with gas are examples of these filler or in-between times. We relate to them quite differently than we do to the "important" happenings. The problem is that the overwhelming bulk of our existence is taken up by these filler moments. If we relate to them as if they are unimportant, we taint a great deal of our lives. But what if we can stop differentiating between the filler moments and the important moments? What if you allow yourself to be fully present wherever you are and whatever you're doing, and realize that these moments are all important? In fact, it turns out that whatever you're doing is the most important thing in the world for you when you are doing it, because that is the only reality of your life at that moment.

In *The Zen Commandments*, Dean Sluyter puts it this way: "We think of the time we spend walking down the corridor from office A to office B as intermission, dead time, mere connective tissue. But there is no intermission. The show never stops. Every moment is the only moment."

In an effort to bring me into the 20th century (yes, I do realize it's the 21st century), my wife recently bought me a cell phone. I needed to have it serviced at the Verizon store. So, here I am, standing in line at the store waiting for my turn. There were three different lines and, although none were particularly long, they all appeared not to be moving. It was hot and I had several other errands to run before getting back to my office. I continued to wait but realized my impatience was growing. Glancing at my watch frequently and doing a modified version of huffing and puffing, I tuned into thoughts such as, "This is ridiculous!" and "There's got to be a better system!" Feeling aggravated and as if this was a big waste of my time, I entertained the idea of leaving the store.

At that moment, the thought came to me, "I could die waiting in this line!" That thought led to a cascade of other thoughts leading to the following scenario: Suppose I did die while waiting in line at the Verizon store and was dead and buried for a year. Then, magically, I was returned to the status of the living and was transposed to the exact spot where I had died. In other words, after being dead for a year, I suddenly find myself very much alive and waiting in line at the Verizon store. This time, I have a whole different feeling and appreciation of that moment. It's as if, "Wow, isn't this great? I'm in line at the Verizon store!" Now, I notice what's happening. People trying to make decisions as they check out the new phones they're thinking about buying. Four or five people talking on cell phones. A couple of excited kids looking at everything. Store employees trying their best to do their jobs in the midst of growing lines of customers. Bold, beautiful colors everywhere. Blues, reds, greens, purples, and yellows. Wow, look at those colors. And people of all sizes, shapes, and colors. "Isn't this amazing? I'm alive and well and standing in line at the Verizon store!"

Now, I'm seeing it through the eyes of a child. These aren't just filler moments until I can get to something that's enjoyable or important. Now, I'm happy standing in line at the Verizon store. It's all grist for the happiness mill. Every moment is the only moment. The show never stops.

Just Passin' Through

The philosopher Montaigne wrote:

How absurd to anguish over our passing...it is equally mad to weep because we shall not be alive a
hundred years from now and to weep because we
were not alive a hundred years ago.

My brother Rip manufactures magnets with various sayings
on them. You know, the kind that stick to your refrigerator. He
came up with the idea of "Just Passin' Through" magnets that are
customized for different areas of the country. Airport shops and
truck stops carry them. For example, "Just Passin' Through Las
Vegas" or "Just Passin' Through San Francisco." They are collecti-
bles, the same way you might get a t-shirt from Bermuda, a little
souvenir of your passage. I like the idea. Just passin' through.
Isn't that what we're all doing? Just passin' through. Just passin'
through life.

I think people unanimously agree that every year passes by
more quickly than the previous year. I often say to myself, "It's
later than it's ever been," to remind myself how quickly time is passing. I know that I'm just passin' through, trying to enjoy the ride,
have fun, help others, and be a decent and loving human being.
This is my turn. Everybody gets a turn. Those who haven't will get
their turn later. But this is my turn. I'm just passin' through and I'm
going to make the best of it. It's not about fame or fortune for me.
It's about the day to day stuff. Hot soup, work, writing, running,
friends and family, discovery, faith, and the sacred unknown.

Bob Dylan wrote a song called "Shooting Star." He sings, "I
seen a shooting star tonight and thought of you," and later, "I seen
a shooting star tonight and thought of me." That's kind of how I
see it. You and I are like these wonderful shooting stars that quickly move through the sky brightening it on their journey. Shooting

stars with the backdrops of the sky and millions of other stars, seemingly less bright and stationary. It's not yet their turn to shoot.

We don't have time to waste. It's later than it's ever been. We've had our share of misery and sorrow. That's part of it too. But to have this opportunity to be alive is a magnificent thing. We're here and now. We're alive and taking our turn. We waited an eternity for this. We're just passin' through and we're thankful for the opportunity.

Big Fred

I used to have an upstairs neighbor, an old, overweight ex-boxer with bad knees, who worked as a janitor. Fred would generally come home with his groceries, a couple of six-packs, and a stack of lottery tickets while I was in the middle of my evening meditation. Through my door I would hear his labored breathing and the clanking of his beer bottles as he struggled up the stairs. At first I tried to ignore it. Then, as the contradiction grew more embarrassing, came annoyance – I would jump up and help him, but resent the fact that my practice had once again been interrupted. Because I'm a slow learner, it took a few weeks before I realized, This *is* the practice. If I have to sit cross-legged on a cushion to experience boundlessness, that's a boundary. Hauling beer up the stairs is the meditation, and Big Fred is the teacher.
-Dean Sluyter

Big Fred is exactly what happens in life. We have expectations of how everything should unfold. We'd like people to say and do certain things. We'd like to be able to write the script for our lives and for what happens in our day to day interactions and events. If we were writing the script, our meditation time would not be interrupted by Big Fred. We try to control what we can and who we can, but eventually realize that doing so is a recipe for unhappiness. So what do we do with Big Fred and everything that he represents? Wars, terrorism, earthquakes, disasters, tragedies, crime, rudeness, lewdness, mistreatment, abandonment, insecurity, frustration, disappointment and the like – all things we didn't quite bargain for.

According to Zorba the Greek, we have to embrace "the whole catastrophe." We can't just take love, friendships, family, rapture, generosity, kindness, and beauty. The world is exactly what it is. Does it really need to be different in order for you to be happy? You can be different and that's about all you're capable of controlling. Let go of expecting the world to be the way you desire and stop fighting the natural ebb and flow of life. Learn to be at ease and never surprised by the whole catastrophe.

The word "amen" is of Hebrew derivation and is translated as meaning "so be it" or "so it is." In Hebrew, it also means truth or truly. We usually say it after prayers. To say amen to is to approve warmly or heartily agree. It is to sanction fully. We need not be restricted to saying it only in prayers. We can say amen to life. We can say amen to the whole ball of wax, to the whole catastrophe. It is so. It is that. It is exactly what it is. Truth. Isness. Embracing life is a key part of the happiness solution. When Pope John Paul II died in 2005, it was widely reported that the last word he said right before he died was "amen."

What's the Point?

On a scale of 1-10, rate your level of happiness. Ten is very happy and one is markedly unhappy. Give your happiness level a number. Do it now, before you read any further. By way of example, let's say you gave yourself a seven. Now, think about what a 10 would be. What would have to happen for your rating to change to a 10? What changes would have to occur in your life? What would you need to do to begin engineering those changes?

Here's what I'd like you to do. If you gave yourself a seven, ask yourself, "What do I need to do to get to a seven-and-a-half?" That's your assignment. I want you to move your happiness level up a half point. That's it. Don't try to go from a seven to a 10 in one leap. Just focus on doing what you need to do in order to obtain seven-and-a-half. I'm pretty sure you can be successful at doing that. When you've achieved and sustained the seven-and-a-half level, describe what an eight would be like. Keep concentrating on the differences between those half points of happiness, and use all your resources to continue raising your happiness level. A half point at a time. It's very doable.

After you figure out what's required to move that half-point, get started quickly. Action is essential. You remember that old Nike advertising campaign that was brilliant in its simplicity – "Just do it!" It wasn't, "Just think about doing it!" Get started now. Move up a half-a-point. Just do it. And if you eventually get to 10, think about 10 ½. Not because you're never satisfied, but because you're alive, curious, grateful, and capable.

> When you get to the top of the mountain,
> keep climbing.
> -Zen Proverb

Make It Happen

We learn to feel helpless and unhappy. Sometimes we learn this as little children. Sometimes as adolescents or young adults. We feel like victims. We feel impotent, trapped, powerless, and afraid. This can go on for a lifetime. In *What Happy People Know*, Dan Baker describes "learned helplessness."

In one of the most important psychological experiments of the last 100 years, young university professor Martin Seligman placed dogs, one at a time, in sealed boxes, from which there was no escape. He placed other dogs in open boxes that did allow escape. Then both sets of dogs were subjected to mild electrical shocks from the floors of their boxes. The dogs in the open boxes quickly learned to jump out. The dogs that had no possibility of escape, however, soon gave up trying to get away from the shocks and laid down, passively accepting their fates. They had learned to feel helpless.

The same dogs were then individually placed in two-compartment boxes, with one side safe from shock. The dogs that had previously been in the open boxes quickly learned to escape the shocks by going to the safe compartments. However, most of the dogs that had already learned to feel helpless stayed in the compartments that shocked them, whining with misery but passively accepting their pain.

A key ingredient of the happiness solution is accepting freedom of choice. Accepting responsibility for your own life. Don't be one of Seligman's passive dogs.

It's later than it's ever been. That's right. Today is _____. You fill in the date. Here's my advice. Show up for your own life. In *The Iceman Cometh* by Eugene O'Neill, the depressed patrons of Harry Hope's Bar numb themselves as they wait and wait for the annual arrival of Hickey. Each year, Hickey provides some measure of relief from their ennui, while ultimately attempting to get them to wake from their collective stupor. Stop waiting for Godot. Stop waiting for Hickey. Stop the "what ifs" and the "yes buts." Stop the "if onlys." Stop the "I should haves," "I could haves," and "if only I would haves." Just stop it and show up for your own life.

Stop "I can't" and "I don't know how." Stop "poor me," just stop it now. Stop blaming and finding faults and holding on to anger, resentment, and guilt. It takes more work and energy to be unhappy than it does to be happy. Start today. Start right now. Be proactive in choosing happiness over unhappiness. Your happiness is your responsibility. It's not too late to create more meaning and joy. When Thoreau finally left Walden Pond in 1847, he explained his departure by saying he had "several more lives to live."

Being productive in a way that means something to you is vital. J.D. Salinger's Holden Caulfield became "The Catcher In The Rye" to help give his life meaning and to feel fulfilled. He misunderstood the song lyrics "when a body meet a body comin' through the rye" and heard them as "when a body catch a body comin' through the rye." So he decided he wanted to be in the field and catch any little kids who were about to fall over the cliff.

Are you being productive enough? Become a manufacturer of happiness. Approach your life whole-heartedly, not half-baked. Develop a positive outlook and bring optimism and zest to your daily activities and encounters. Get involved. Take your passion. Make it happen.

> There are only two ways to live your life.
> One is as though nothing is a miracle.
> The other is as though everything is a miracle.
> -Albert Einstein

Learned Happiness

One day during a speaking tour, Albert Einstein's driver, who often sat at the back of the hall during his lectures, remarked that he could probably give the lecture himself, having heard it so many times. Sure enough, at the next stop on the tour, Einstein and the driver switched places, with Einstein sitting at the back, wearing his driver's uniform.

Having delivered a flawless lecture, the driver was asked a difficult question by a member of the audience. "Well, the answer to that question is quite simple," he casually replied. "I bet my driver, sitting in the back there, could answer it."

Sometimes, complicated questions can have relatively simple answers. In fact, the question, "How can I be happier?" is an example of that. The answer is to practice the principles of happiness as outlined in this book. If you wanted to be a better golfer, you'd take lessons and practice what you learned. You'd remember to watch the ball, keep your head down, and focus on the mechanics of your back swing, swing, and follow through. You'd hit thousands of balls at the driving range and keep practicing. Eventually, it would feel more natural. Same thing with happiness.

If happiness is your goal, you need to understand what factors the studies on happiness have determined to be directly related to increasing it. Now that these factors have been identified for you, the next step is making a vigorous and concerted effort to create the new patterns of thinking and behavior that lead to happiness. In other words, you are taking the research findings on what creates happiness and incorporating those findings into your everyday life. This is "learned happiness" and it is eminently doable. At first it may seem strange or awkward, but if you keep at it, positive results are inevitable.

Just about every story in this book offers a principle of happiness to be practiced daily. Our natural state of being is happiness.

Infants and toddlers exude happiness until they learn how to be unhappy. We've learned our lessons well.

> We have become geniuses in pinpointing all that's difficult and bad in our lives and the world around us. The media reflect and reinforce that bias. The reward for such studious vigilance results in continual stress, discomfort, and anxiety. We set ourselves up for unhappiness rather than for peace or comfort.
> -Barry Neil Kaufman

Now, I'm asking you to become a genius in pinpointing what you have learned about producing happiness. I want you to set yourself up for joy, serenity, peace-of-mind, contentment, optimism, well-being, and fulfillment. Read all the stories again. Make a list of what will bring you happiness. Digest it. Absorb it. Live it. Indeed, happiness can be learned. I care deeply that you get it, and live it.

Who made the world?
Who made the swan, and the black bear?
Who made the grasshopper?
This grasshopper, I mean –
the one who has flung herself out of the grass,
the one who is eating sugar out of my hand,
who is moving her jaws back and forth instead of up and down –
who is gazing around with her enormous and complicated eyes.
Now she lifts her pale forearms and thoroughly washes her face.
Now she snaps her wings open, and floats away.
I don't know exactly what a prayer is.
I do know how to pay attention,
how to fall down into the grass,
how to kneel down in the grass,
how to be idle and blessed,
how to stroll through the fields,
which is what I have been doing all day.
Tell me, what else should I have done?
Doesn't everything die at last, and too soon?

Tell me, what is it you plan to do
with your one wild and precious life?
-*The Summer Day* by Mary Oliver

Notes

Page 17: "Caught Between a Rock and a Hard Place" used material as reported by *The Associated Press*.

Page 20: "Schrodinger's Cat" experiment design as summarized on www.anecdotage.com

Page 72: See www.jimrohn.com

Page 165: The material for "Baba Yaga" was gathered on numerous websites including www.en.wikipedia.org

Permissions from:

Parabola to use stories cited in "Henny-Penny" and "Coyote."

City Lights Books to use stories from *The Old Ways* by Gary Snyder.

Beacon Press to use poems from *New and Selected Poems* by Mary Oliver.

Works Cited

Abelson, Robert P., et. al. <u>Experiments With People: Revelations From Social Psychology</u>. Mahwah: Lawrence Erlbaum Associates, 2004.

Adler, Jerry. "In Search of the Spiritual." <u>Newsweek</u> 05 Sep 2005: 46-64.

Bach, Richard. <u>Jonathan Livingston Seagull</u>. New York: Avon, 1973.

Baker, Dan. <u>What Happy People Know: How the New Science of Happiness Can Change Your Life For the Better</u>. New York: St. Martin's Press, 2003.

Balter, Michael. "The Seeds of Civilization." <u>Smithsonian</u> 36.2 (2005): 68-74.

Boman, Steve. "Racing Against the Clock." <u>GeezerJock</u> Summer 2005: 17.

Borysenko, Joan. <u>Minding the Body, Mending the Mind</u>. New York: Bantam, 1988.

Campbell, Joseph. <u>The Masks of God: Oriental Mythology</u>. New York: Penguin Books, 1977.

Campbell, Joseph. <u>The Masks of God: Primitive Mythology</u>. New York: Penguin Books, 1984.

Carlson, Richard. <u>Easier Than You Think</u>. New York: Harper Collins, 2005.

Cooper, Robert. <u>Health and Fitness Excellence</u>. Boston: Houghton Mifflin, 1989.

Dass, Ram. <u>Still Here: Embracing Aging, Changing, and Dying</u>. New York: Riverhead Books, 2000.

Doty, William. "Faces of Death." <u>Parabola</u> 2.1 (1977): 60-65.

Easterbrook, Gregg. "The Real Truth About Money." <u>Time</u> 17 Jan 2005: A32-A34.

Feder, Kenneth L. <u>Frauds, Mysteries and Myths</u>. 4th Edition. New York: McGraw Hill, 2001.

Flora, Carlin. "Happy Hour." <u>Psychology Today</u> 38.1 (2005): 40-50.

Fremantle, Francesca., and Chogyam Trungpa. The Tibetan Book of the Dead. Berkeley: Shambhala Publications, 1975.

Fromm, Erich. Beyond the Chains of Illusion. New York: Simon and Schuster, 1962.

Gettis, Alan. Seven Times Down, Eight Times Up: Landing on Your Feet in an Upside Down World. Victoria: Trafford, 2003.

Gettis, Alan. Sun Faced Haiku, Moon Faced Haiku. Battle Ground: High/Coo Press, 1982.

Hanh, Thich Nhat. No Death No Fear. New York: Riverhead Books, 2002.

Hansen, Linda. "The Journey Toward Hope." UU World Sep/Oct 2003: 27-33.

Kaufman, Barry Neil. Happiness Is a Choice. New York: Fawcett Columbine, 1991.

Keen, Sam. To a Dancing God. New York: Harper and Row, 1970.

Keyes, Ken. The Hundredth Monkey. 2nd Edition. St. Mary, KY: Vision Books, 1984.

Kopp, Sheldon. If You Meet the Buddha On the Road, Kill Him! Palo Alto: Science and Behavior Books, 1972.

Koren, Leonard. Wabi-Sabi For Artists, Designers, Poets and Philosophers. Berkeley: Stone Bridge Press, 1994.

Kornfield, Jack. After the Ecstasy, the Laundry: How the Heart Grows Wise on the Spiritual Path. New York: Bantam Books, 2000.

Leary, Mark. "Get Over Yourself!" Psychology Today 37.4 (2004): 62-65.

Lemonick, Michael. "The Biology of Joy." Time 17 Jan 2005: A12-A17.

Levine, Stephen and Ondrea. Who Dies? : An Investigation of Conscious Living and Conscious Dying. New York: Anchor, 1989.

Luciani, Joseph J. The Power of Self-Coaching: The Five Essential Steps to Creating the Life You Want. Hoboken: John Wiley and Sons, 2004.

Menahem, Sam. All Your Prayers Are Answered. Lincoln: Writer's Digest, 2000.

Miller, Timothy. How to Want What You Have. New York: Henry Holt and Co., 1995.

Oliver, Mary. New and Selected Poems. Boston: Beacon Press, 1992.

Paul, Pamela. "The Power to Uplift." Time 17 Jan 2005: A46-A48.

Peterson, Christopher., and Martin Seligman. <u>Character Strengths and Virtues: A Handbook and Classification</u>. Oxford: Oxford University Press, 2004.

Ralston, Aron. <u>Between a Rock and a Hard Place</u>. New York: Atria, 2005.

Ray, Oakley. "How the Mind Hurts and Heals the Body." <u>American Psychologist</u> 59.1 (2004): 29-40.

Riviere, Joan. <u>Sigmund Freud: Collected Papers (Volume 4)</u>. New York: Basic Books, 1959.

Ryan, M.J. <u>The Happiness Makeover: How to Teach Yourself to Be Happy and Enjoy Every Day</u>. New York: Random House, 2005.

Rymer, Russ. "Saving the Music Tree." <u>Smithsonian</u> 35.1 (2004): 52-63.

Schwarz-Bart, Andre. <u>The Last of the Just</u>. New York: Bantam, 1976.

Seligman, Martin. <u>Authentic Happiness</u>. New York: Free Press, 2004.

Sheler, Jeffrey. "The Power of Prayer." <u>U.S. News and World Report</u> 20 Dec 2004: 52-54.

Sluyter, Dean. <u>The Zen Commandments</u>. New York: Jeremy P. Tarcher/Putnam, 2001.

Snyder, Gary. <u>He Who Hunted Birds In His Father's Village: The Dimensions of a Haida Myth</u>. Bolinas: Grey Fox Press, 1979.

Snyder, Gary. <u>The Old Ways</u>. San Francisco: City Light Books, 1977.

Sohl, Robert., and Audrey Carr. <u>The Gospel According to Zen</u>. New York: Mentor, 1970.

Southern, Vanessa. <u>This Piece of Eden</u>. Boston: Skinner House, 2001.

Stark, John. "American Wabi-Sabi." <u>Body + Soul</u> Jul/Aug 2004: 76-80, 100.

Steadman, Ralph. <u>Sigmund Freud</u>. New York: Paddington Press, 1979.

The Dalai Lama., and Howard C. Cutler. <u>The Art of Happiness</u>. New York: Riverhead, 1998.

Travers, P.L. "Henny-Penny." <u>Parabola</u> IV.4 (1979): 79-80.

VanDerPost, Laurens. <u>The Lost World of the Kalahari</u>. New York: Harcourt, 1977.

Wallis, Claudia. "The New Science of Happiness." <u>Time</u> 17 Jan 2005: A2-A9.

Walsh, Roger. <u>Essential Spirituality</u>. New York: John Wiley and Sons, 1999.

Wernick, Robert. "In Search of William Tell." <u>Smithsonian</u> 35.5 (2004): 70-78.